Daddy, We Never Knew You!

The Story of God 2.0

R.A. Varghese

TESTAMENT  Book House

228 Park Ave S
PMB 19611
New York, New York 10003-1502

ISBN 978-1-7364447-4-0

Copyright © 2021 by R.A. Varghese

All rights reserved. No part of this publication may be reproduced, stored in a retrieval system, or transmitted, in any form or by any means, electronic, mechanical, photocopying, recording, or otherwise, without the prior permission of Roy Abraham Varghese.

Published May 2021

For my father, M. Abraham Varghese (1933-1992)

TABLE OF CONTENTS

Prologue – *Lover, Love Letter, Love Story* 1

A Time for Truth – *The Revolution Breaks Out* 7

Once Upon a Time – *God 1.0 and THE Promise* 13
    B.C. 13
    A.D. 17

The Fullness of Time – *Proclaiming God 2.0* 19
    The Father Sends Us His Son and His Holy Spirit 19
    The Father as Source of the Son and the Holy Spirit 24
    The Father Revealed by Jesus 25
    Abba as Fundamental to Understanding and Interacting with God ... 25
    Can We Call God "Abba"? 28
    Who is Prodigal in the Parable? 29
    Our Father 30
    The Voice of the Father 30

Time Out – *Exploring God 2.0* 31
    God is Infinite Spirit 32
    How We Know That Jesus Is God Incarnate 33
    Why We Say That God Is Trinity 40

Time for a Change – *Discovering God 2.0* 45
    Prodigal Father 46
    Leaving 47
    Returning 51
    Backstory 52
    ***Abba* Father** 54
    Birth of a New Race 54

Our Father 57
  "There is Nothing I Shall Lack" 57
  The Promised Land 63

A Time for Action – *Homo Sapiens 2.0* 65
  From Knowing to Doing 65
  A Map of GodSpace 73
  Parallel Universe – A Portal to the Promised Land 73
  Badlands – *Sin* 74
  Highlands – *Prayer* 77
  Lowlands – *Worry* 79
  Mother of All Who Keep God's Commandments 85
  Prayer to Father, Son, or Holy Spirit or to the Trinity? 87

Time is of the Essence – *Consummating the Revolution* 91
  Our Personal Consecration to the Father 91
  Humankind's Consecration to the Father through a Feast of *Abba*,
    Our Father, the Father of All Humanity 92
  Why a Feast of the Father is Required in Our Worship 94
  An Ecumenical Feast for All Humankind 95

Face Time – *An Affair of the Heart*

Epilogue – *Living Happily Ever After* 97

<u>Appendix 1</u>
What About Anthropomorphism, Patriarchalism, Sexism and Atheism? 101

<u>Appendix 2</u>
Does *Abba* Mean Daddy or Father and Is That Really an Issue? 107

<u>Appendix 3</u>
Human Heart, Divine Heart, Heart2heart 109

R.A. Varghese is the author and/or editor of sixteen books on the interface of science, philosophy, and religion. His *Cosmos, Bios, Theos*, included contributions from 24 Nobel Prize-winning scientists. *Time* magazine called *Cosmos* "the year's most intriguing book about God." *Cosmic Beginnings and Human Ends*, a subsequent work, won a Templeton Book Prize for "*Outstanding Books in Science and Natural Theology.*" His *The Wonder of the World* was endorsed by leading thinkers include two Nobelists and was the subject of an Associated Press story. He co-authored *There is a God—How the World's Most Notorious Atheist Changed His Mind* with Antony Flew (a book translated into Spanish, Portuguese, Korean, Russian, and Arabic). His most recent work, *The Missing Link* (2013), includes contributions from three Nobel Prize winners and scientists from Oxford, Cambridge, Harvard, and Yale. Varghese was a panelist at the science and religion forum in the Parliament of World Religions held in Chicago in 1993 and an invitee and participant in the Millennium World Peace Summit of Religious and Spiritual Leaders held at the United Nations in August 2000. Varghese has been interviewed on numerous radio and TV shows including *Coast to Coast*. He has also been profiled in different print publications.

"2.0"

Definition – "used to denote a superior
or more advanced version of an original concept"
(Oxford)

"Sigmund Freud, although he was an atheist, understood very clearly what defective fathering can do to belief in God. ... Once a child or youth is disappointed in and loses his or her respect for their earthly father, they will have a harder time believing in their heavenly Father. ... In just about every case, the atheists had defective relationships with their fathers."[1]
Psychologist *Paul C. Vitz*

"The most popular prayer in the world is addressed to 'Our Father who art in heaven.' It is possible that man's earliest prayers were addressed to the same heavenly father."[2]
Comparative Religion theorist *Mircea Eliade*

"The name 'father' is applied to the Supreme Being in every single area of the primitive culture when he is addressed or appealed to. It seems, therefore, that we may consider it primeval and proper to the oldest primitive culture. We find it in the form 'father' simply, also in the individual form ('my father') and the collective ('our father')."[3]
Stone Age and Hunter-Gatherer anthropologist *Wilhelm Schmidt*

"Our father, who created and set in order and knows all forms, all worlds."
Rig Veda (1200- 900 B.C.), the first major work in an Indo-European language and the holiest scripture of Hinduism

"Is not this your father, who gave you being, who made you, by whom you subsist?"
Deuteronomy 32:6.

"To Do the Will of Our Father in Heaven: Toward a Partnership between Jews and Christians. After nearly two millennia of mutual hostility and alienation, we Orthodox Rabbis who lead communities, institutions and seminaries in Israel, the United States and Europe recognize the historic opportunity now before us. We seek to do the will of our Father in Heaven by accepting the hand offered to us by our Christian brothers and sisters. Jews and Christians must work together as partners to address the moral challenges of our era." *Orthodox Rabbinic Statement on Christianity*[4]

"The Our Father begins with a great consolation: we are allowed to say "Father." This one word contains the whole history of redemption."[5]
Poet *Reinhold Schneider*

"I give praise to you, Father, Lord of heaven and earth, for although you have hidden these things from the wise and the learned you have revealed them to the childlike."
Matthew 11:25

"That you may be children of your heavenly Father." *Matthew* 5:45

"But the hour is coming, and is now here, when true worshipers will worship the Father in Spirit and truth; *and indeed the Father seeks such people to worship him.*"
John 4:23

Prologue
Lover, Love Letter, Love Story

Have you ever been in love? Have you felt your thoughts become tears? Have you heard your heart break into song?

And what if the one you love is Love Itself, the Source of all joy, the Creator of all?

And what if it was Love Itself that loved you first, that loved you into being, that asks only that you offer your love as well?

This is our story here, a "Once upon a time" tale that ends "happily ever after" if so we choose.

It is the story of a Father whose love is infinitely prodigal, prodigal in the sense of "extravagant", and who is our *Abba*, our infinitely tender loving Father for whom even the word "Daddy" is not affectionate enough (although it's a start!).

He is our Lover whose love letters WE are. And if we love him back then our life becomes the ultimate love story for we are drawn into the infinite-eternal Love Story we call God.

For God is a beginningless, endless Act of Love of the Lover (the Father), the Beloved (the Son) and the Co-Beloved (the Spirit). God is a Trinity of Love, of Three Persons in Love. God is Heart. For to be Heart is to give all of one's being to the Other: to give totally, unconditionally, forever: to love.

There is only one Godhead, one infinite Mind and Will: but it is a Heart and so "possessed" by Three, each possessing it in a particular way: and each seen by us as Heart in its own distinctive relation: the Paternal Heart ("God so loved the world"), the Heart that became man ("Whoever has seen me has seen the Father"), the Heart that fills our hearts ("God sent the spirit of his Son into our hearts, crying out, "Abba, Father!").

R.A. Varghese

Infinite-Eternal Love

Love is the "cause," essence and fruit of the Heart that is the tri-personal God.

Ultimately there is nothing as good, as valuable, as "worth it" as "love": To know all things, to possess all other perfections, but not to love infinitely is to lack fullness of joy.

What is love? It is the self-sacrificing, unconditional giving of one to another, the whole-hearted willing of all that benefits the beloved.

Love in its highest form at the human level – which is the level of spirit – is thus giving, receiving, sharing.

In childbirth, we see how the human parents "give" the gift of human nature to a new "center," a person who is the fruit of their love.

Now the essence of God, the divine essence or nature, is the infinite perfection of an infinite Mind and Will: omnipotence, omniscience, the Good.

This essence is "given" by one divine Person, "received" by another and jointly possessed with a third.

The relationship among them is one of love: total and perfect. It has no beginning, no end. It just IS.

The same divine essence, the same nature, is exercised by the Three in one eternal act of giving, receiving, possessing.

Hence there is one God and Three Persons within that one God.

To summarize: what does God do? God loves.

What does it mean to love? To give.

What kind of giving is the kind of love we find in God? The highest possible kind: the gift of one's nature, the divine nature, the fullness of all perfection.

But to be a gift "worthy of God" it has to be given to the highest possible recipient: to One who is God by receiving the divine Life: Father and Son from all eternity.

And the love between the Two must as well be the highest possible kind of gift: again, a love that bears fruit in One who is God. The Spirit who is Love proceeds from the Father through the Son.

One Person, the Lover, gives all to Another, the Beloved, and the love they share in common, the Co-Beloved, is itself another Person: all in the one divine Mind and Will: all without beginning or end; all in one infinite Act of Love; and, hence, all as One Heart.

How do we know all this? Since God is infinite perfection, God is also infinite love. But God can be infinite love only if there is love *within* God.

Since God is infinite, the love in its origin (the Father), its object (the Son) and its fruit (the Holy Spirit) must likewise be infinite: Three infinite inseparable "centers" that ARE the One.

And in what would such love consist? As we have seen, in a giving, receiving and sharing in full of the divine nature, of all that it means to be God. The divine perfections, this means, are gifted and received, possessed and exercised by the Three. There is only one God: but it is "possessed" by Three, each of whom possesses it in a particular way.

The magnificence and glory that is God, then, is a blazing furnace of love of Lover, Beloved and Co-Beloved.

The Lover is our infinitely Prodigal Father. It is this Father (the divine Paternal Heart) who seeks to draw us into his infinite-eternal Act of Love through the Beloved (the Son, the incarnate Heart) by means of the Co-Beloved (the Spirit, the spiritual Heart dwelling in our hearts).

His Love manifested itself from the beginning of creation.

The Big Bang of Be-ing

To be or not to be? Why is there something and not nothing? How did anything at all come to "be"?

The Universe we live in has trillions of galaxies with quintillions of stars (one quintillion is a billion trillion!). At every level the Universe is bursting with changes from one state to another. How did these processes begin, what keeps them going? Most important: how did they get to be here? Do they have the power to bring themselves into existence? No. For that to happen, they would have to exist before they existed!

In short, the Universe has no power of "creating" itself. Nor does it have any inherent logic of always existing. But nothing can come to be from nothingness. So how did the Universe get here?

The only answer is that it originated from "something" that has the inherent Power of always existing. Something that exists by its very nature.

For something to have a nature of always existing is to have full "control" of its existence: to not depend on anything else for BE-ING: to be self-"powered" with no limit or end! This something is what we mean by God.

As for the rest of us (i.e., the entire Universe), our ability to be, our be-ing, is "powered" entirely by God much as *an electric current can "be" only with a power source.*

God did not simply bring us into being. It is because of him that we *continue to be* just as sunlight continues to be because of the sun. God is what holds the Universe with its laws, properties, agents and history in being at every instant.

We can see our dependence on God at many levels. For instance, his entire cosmos cooperated in the creation of our physical being with countless just-right physical ratios and values:

- *The expansion rate of the universe*: If it was any higher, there would be no time for galaxies to form. If it was lower with the force of gravity being higher, matter would fall back on itself and form one giant lump.
- *The age of the Universe*: It has to be at least 13 billion years old for human life to form. If it was any earlier, there would be no time for the stellar furnaces with its 20 life-essential elements (e.g., iron) to form. If it was any later, the stars would go dim and life would not be possible.
- *The mass of the Universe*: If it was larger, its expansion would be slower; no light elements would form. If it was smaller, the expansion would be faster; no heavy elements would form. In either case, there would be no life.
- *Nature's fundamental constants*: If there was any change in the numerical value of myriad constants such as the strength of the electromagnetic force or the constants that govern the masses of elementary particles and their interactions, life could not form.

Then there is the here and now. Bacteria, plants, animals, the "birds of the air," us – we are all preserved in being not only with various physical parameters but with food sources and the instincts to secure food. And also the right ecosystem. If we were to go into "outer space" without protection, we would perish almost instantly thanks to its vacuum effect, low pressure, lack of oxygen, −100C/+100C temperatures, lethal radiation, meteoroids and so much else.

All this sounds very much like we were "meant" to be here: that the Universe is indeed "home."

All this sounds, in fact, like the action of the Father of whom Jesus of Nazareth spoke: "Look at the birds in the sky; they do not sow or reap, they gather nothing into barns, yet your heavenly Father feeds them."

Psalm 139 comes to mind: "You formed my inmost being …. My very self you know … I was being made in secret, fashioned in the depths of the earth. Your eyes saw me unformed; in your book all are written down; my days were shaped, before one came to be. How precious to me are your designs, O God; how vast the sum of them!" (*Psalm* 139: 13-6).

Everything is mystery and magic, everything is gift, everything is, in fact, the Father speaking his infinite love to us.

To be is to be loved.

"God So Loved the World"

The most famous verse in the Bible tells us: "God so loved the world that he gave his only Son, so that everyone who believes in him might not perish but might have eternal life." (*John* 3:16).

The first part of the sentence, "God so loved the world" explains and gives meaning to our existence. It tells us about our Father's Heart: the Love that brought us into being and rescues us from the mortal danger in which we placed ourselves.

It is the human face of this Lover that we see in his Beloved, the "only Son" who was sent by him to save us from our sins.

Jesus of Nazareth, the Son, is a phenomenon and not an abstract matter of history or biography or even theology. The phenomenon is Jesus here and now doing what his name proclaims: "saving his people." And his "saving" is a story of love – total, unconditional love that he offers every one of us and asks that we show to "the least" among us. No one else ever came with a message of such overwhelming, overpowering, all-embracing, all-pervasive love: asking total surrender, total trust, offering nothing but total love. No one else came as Heart.

Exceptionally holy men had spoken of detachment from the world, of showing compassion to all living beings and of leading a pure life. But none had spoken of actively loving your enemies, of selflessly serving your fellow beings and thereby serving God, of giving up your very life to save your neighbor. The very idea of loving and forgiving your murderers *while* they are driving nails into your flesh is so unthinkable, so unnatural, that it could not have been invented. This is Love itself. This is the phenomenon. This is GOD.

And it was Jesus who told us about the infinite Lover, his Father who is now OUR Father.

It was Jesus who said that to see him was to see the Father.

And it is through Jesus and the Spirit who filled him that we who are love letters of the Father can become his love stories.

A Time for Truth
The Revolution Breaks Out

This is a story of the ultimate revolution – the revelation of the true nature of things, of you and me and the world, of our place in the grand scheme. It is the revelation that there is a Creator of all things, that this Creator, God, is "our" Father, that the purpose of life is to become children of the Father, our hearts one with the divine Heart, and that we are called to live from this moment forward in the Kingdom of the Father, GodSpace.

The story began "once upon a time" at the dawn of history with the creation of the physical universe and then of life-forms including those conscious, thinking beings we call homo sapiens. But somewhere along the way, there was a collision, a power failure, a death. The death of a family, the human family.

All this we will consider in due course. But the net effect of this event was an unbridgeable gulf between Creator and creature. Humankind in every era sought to return to "the way we were." This we see in the universal practice of sacrifice. In parallel, the Creator sought to free humanity from its self-inflicted bondage. This is what we see in the proclamations of prophets and the miracles of the Holy Ones.

The Coming of Jesus – the Climax of the Divine Outreach

We will be revisiting all these happenings as we proceed. But our concern at the moment is the climax of the divine outreach to the race gone astray. So we will jump ahead to the coming of Jesus of Nazareth, the Messiah of Israel, eternal Word of God and Redeemer of the human race. The whole identity and mission of Jesus of Nazareth centered on the Father. Jesus addressed God only as Father. The Father is "father" because Jesus as Word is his infinite-eternal Son. And the Love between Father and Son is such that it bears fruit as Another, the Holy Spirit.

The Father revealed by Jesus was:

- prodigal in his limitless love,
- more intimate than any earthly parent and therefore called *Abba* (the affectionate Aramaic expression for one's own father) and, above all,
- "our" Father meeting all our needs all the time and drawing us into GodSpace, the protection and provision of his Providence.

Henceforth, we cannot see God except as the Father who makes us his children through his Son and in his Holy Spirit. The Father is infinite perfection, majestic beyond comprehension, and yet he is infinitely intimate, inconceivably more intimate than even the most affectionate of our expressions – be it "daddy" or "father" – can convey.

And yet, two millennia later, this infinitely loving Father, as also the treasure-house he bequeaths us, remain a secret! Among Christians we hear about Jesus and the Holy Spirit but very little about the Father who "so loved" us as to send his Son and his Spirit for our salvation and sanctification. The Christian calendar has Christmas, Easter and Pentecost but no commemoration of the Father's acts. He is truly the Missing (divine) Person.

In our story here we will discover the three-fold dimensions of the Father revealed by Jesus: prodigal Father, *Abba* Father, Our Father.

We will become children of this Father living with his Life, our hearts embedded in his Paternal Heart. And we will enter GodSpace.

These are the three truths that constitute the revolutionary revelation and that we explore here:

1. God is our Father.
2. We are called to be his children, through his Son and in his Holy Spirit, in the fullest possible sense for all eternity.
3. We are offered, in this life, a shelter from all possible storms and a never-ending Power Source for all that we need – GodSpace.

What Jesus Revealed

With one exception, when he was citing Psalm 22, Jesus directly addressed God only as Father as seen over 60 times in the Synoptic Gospels and some 100 times in the Gospel of John.

Jesus tells us that "true" worship must be directed to the Father.

The Father Jesus revealed was prodigal, i.e., extravagant, in his love and generosity.

Even more astonishingly, Jesus calls God *Abba*, the intimate and affectionate Aramaic term for one's own father – a first in religious history. He tells us we are all called to become children of this *Abba* – an assimilation made possible by the Spirit of Father and the Son – and thus live with him forever.

Jesus further tells us that he is "Our" Father, who insists on meeting our every need and who urges us to turn our lives over to him. As his children, in this world we are all invited to live in the Kingdom of the Father, GodSpace, the divine Paternal Heart, Heaven here-and-now.

This is why we say that the Father unveiled to us is the Prodigal Father, Abba Father, Our Father.

We speak of this as the ultimate revolution simply because it changes the entire understanding of our origin and destiny. It transfigures our thoughts and feelings, our plans and perspectives, our choices and actions. For the first time, we see that we are dealing not with a hostile universe or a distant deity but with an infinitely loving, constantly present, ever-providing Lover – the Father. And we live as his children in his Kingdom on earth as it is in Heaven.

Father-Sent

We learn too that Jesus is the incarnation or human embodiment of the Father's eternal Son who the Father sends to us because he "so" loves us. And that the Father through the Son sends us the divine Fruit of their infinite Love, their Holy Spirit.

There is a reason for the Father's sending of his Son and his Spirit. Through the incarnation, death and resurrection of his Son on our behalf, the Father offers us redemption from our sins. Through the subsequent sending of his Holy Spirit into our "hearts," the Father makes us his children, adopted brothers and sisters of his Son, who can live with him forever. We can only become his children if we live with his own Life – his Spirit – who are thereby able to call him "Abba."

This revelation was a revolution at the level of knowledge. But, just as important, it was a revolution in terms of our relationship with God and the way in which we lead our lives. It was a revolution of the heart. To discover the Father is also to discover our identity as his children who live in GodSpace.

Nothing will ever be the same again

God, from our standpoint, will never be the same again. He is no longer an impersonal abstraction, a remote sovereign or an extra-cosmic Force. He is

God 2.0 – our prodigal Father, present with us here and now, engaging us Heart2heart, fulfilling our deepest desires, leading us to eternal ecstasy.

And yet, surprisingly, the revolution of seeing and experiencing God as "Father" seems to have had a decisive impact only in the first Christian century. This is surprising because the constant awareness and trust in the Father is reflected only in the New Testament writings. It was less pronounced in later writings.

Everything in Jesus' teaching was centered on the Father. But this emphasis is hardly evident in later Christianity.

Perfect Storm – Discovering the Inner Life of God While Fighting for Your Life

There was an understandable reason for this colossal oversight. The disciples of Jesus faced the challenge of consolidating the whole new body of revelation he unveiled: the incarnation of the Son; the sending of the Spirit; the indwelling of Father, Son and Holy Spirit within the One Godhead.

Jesus revealed that within God there are Three Persons. God is Three-in-One, the Trinity.

The Father is the source-less Source of the divinity in the Trinity. He gives all that he is (other than being Father) to the Son from all eternity. The love of Father and Son bears fruit as a Third Person, the Holy Spirit – again from all eternity.

The intuition of an eternal relationship within the Godhead was, in fact, shared by all the major pre-Christian religions of India, China and Israel. It was confirmed by Jesus, the human locus of the eternal Son.

The first Christian centuries were necessarily focused on exploring the divine identity of the Son and the Spirit; the "structure" of the Trinity; and the Incarnation of the Son. This treasure-house of truth had to be explored, clarified and defined.

It was the theological equivalent of discovering Relativity and Quantum Physics and then mapping out a new vision of the physical world.

It created the "perfect storm". The followers of Jesus in the first seven hundred years of Christianity had to draw out a coherent body of doctrine from the primordial revelation. They had to "live" the faith in their worship. They had to propagate the truths handed down to them to all the world. And all this in the midst of persecution, poverty and heresy!

Son and Spirit

The incarnation of the Son of God in Jesus of Nazareth is where the final revelation began. But it took seven centuries to map the infrastructure underlying this hard fact. Then there was Jesus' teaching that he had to leave so that "the Father" can "give you another Advocate to be with you always, The Spirit of truth." (*John 14:16*). Jesus' ascension into Heaven was followed by the fiery descent of the Holy Spirit and the birth of the Church. It took centuries more to grasp the role and action of the divine Spirit.

The necessary focus on the Son and the Spirit is reflected in the fact that the principal sacred celebrations of Christianity are Christmas (the incarnation of the Son), Easter (the resurrection of the Son) and Pentecost (the descent of the Holy Spirit).

Father-less

But there is a "Missing Person" in this mix – the Father! There is no corresponding commemoration of the Father's acts in salvation history.

The absence of the Father in the Christian calendar reflects a deeper problem. The Father has faded out of the Christian consciousness.

Of course, the "Our Father" remains the prayer of choice for Christian. But, too often, the prayer becomes a mechanical recitation, a formality. Many liturgies too are directed to the Father but again these remain abstract affirmations and not a living reality. And although personal prayers are often addressed to the Father, they lack the essential next steps of becoming children of the Father and entering GodSpace.

For most Christians, to live their faith means being "born again" or "filled with the Holy Spirit" or baptized or partaking of the Lord's Supper/Eucharist. There is nothing wrong with this of course. These are, in fact, essential elements of becoming children of the Father.

But essential as they are, they all revolve around something more fundamental: the Father. And the Father is missing!

That is to say, in practical terms, the center of gravity seems to have shifted almost entirely to the Son and the Spirit and remained there.

The freshness and real-world immediacy, the all-pervasive presence and transformational power of the Father revealed by Jesus are rarely recognized.

This is a tragedy because the Father is the Source and Goal of creation. It is a tragedy because the purpose of the salvific saga is to become children of the Father.

And in practical terms it is a tragedy above all because we have deprived ourselves of the Power and the Protection, the Peace and the Joy of GodSpace. It is here that the Father revealed by Jesus will transform our lives if we consciously turn to him at all times as shown by his Son. Our hearts are restless until they rest in his Paternal Heart.

Homeward Bound

But there is no need to worry. Once we recognize what was left behind, we simply have to retrace our steps to Jesus' revolutionary revelation. There we discover our infinitely loving Father.

The discovery begins with Jesus' revelation that the hour is "now here" when "true worshipers will worship the Father." We then proceed to the three-fold dimensions of the Father revealed by Jesus: prodigal Father, *Abba* Father, Our Father.

It is he who feeds the birds in the sky and has counted "the hairs" of our heads. It is he who brought all things into being for us, he who rushes out to embrace us every time we turn our backs on him, he who has made us the heirs of his eternal Kingdom.

Our story is a journey into GodSpace that begins with the Prodigal Father who shows himself to be "our" Father and leads us into his Kingdom "on earth as it is in heaven."

This is the ultimate revolution which is also the ultimate love story, the ultimate "affair of the heart." The Father who loved us into being, the Father whom we abandoned, has sent us his Son and his Spirit so that we might be able to return to him if so we choose. Regardless of what we choose, the Son gave up his life so that we might live. Such is the Love of the Father, manifested by his Son and delivered by his Spirit.

Born again in his Son, filled with his Spirit, let us return to the *Abba* who awaits us with robe and ring and feast.

Once Upon a Time
God 1.0 and THE Promise

B.C.

From the time of the hunter-gatherers through the most ancient organized religions, there was a consensus that there was a divine order "behind the scenes."

Polytheism and idolatry was all-pervasive in the secondary cultures of the ancient world. But the most ancient peoples across the world, the hunter-gatherers and those who still lived in a Stone Age culture, believed in a High God that went beyond all other gods – in many cases a supreme God.

The anthropologist of religion Ninian Smart observes that among these societies, "Ruling over the world ..., there is - high above in the sky, but not of the sky - some kind of supreme Being. ... The existence of such conceptions among folk as far apart as the inhabitants of Tierra del Fuego [at the Southern end of Chile] and the Arctic is a significant indication that primitive religion... possesses sophisticated ideas about the beginning and creation of the world, and about a supreme architect of the world."[1]

John Mbiti, a leading authority on African religion, says that of the 300 main traditional religions, "In all these societies, without a single exception, people have a notion of God as the Supreme Being."[2]

Hinduism had polytheism but there was a clear sense of a supreme godhead behind the various deities. Likewise in China, polytheism and later Taoism and Confucianism co-existed with the belief in a supreme being, Shang Di. The same was true of the Persians. So the major organized religions held to the idea of a Supreme God that grounded the profusion of secondary deities.

The religion of the people of Israel was unique to the ancient world. Despite occasional forays into polytheism and idolatry, the Israelites became staunch monotheists. Unlike any other prior religious document, the Hebrew Bible is an account of the interaction between the divine Mind and a specific race of people over a period of thousands of years. And crucial to this interaction is the deity's insistence on monotheism ("Thou shalt have no other gods before me."). This insistence is absolute. So much so, idolatry and polytheism are punishable by death.

Nowhere in ancient history do we find anything remotely similar. God is telling a people that they shall have no other god. The Shema is to be recited daily. Monotheism had to be drummed into the human mind because of the constant temptation to wander away. And clearly the "treatment" worked, for the Jews by the time of Jesus were as staunchly monotheist as it is possible for a people to be.

The supreme God of ancient religion is what we might call God 1.0. And it reached its climax in the people of Israel.

In addition to their belief in the Divine, the most ancient religions believed that the divinely instituted sacred order of the Universe had been breached by human evil and that humanity had to perform sacrifice in expiation. "Sacrifice" means "make sacred" and it was believed that the Divine was present where sacrifice was performed. Fundamental to sacrifice was the idea of the blood covenant, blood being shed in atonement so as to bring about a restoration of union with the Divine. The blood of the sacrificial animal was identified with its life and this life was being offered up for the redemption of the offerors.

Sacrifice began at the very dawn of human history with the hunter-gatherers. The focus on atonement, covenant and communion was especially apparent in the elaborate ceremonies of the largest organized religions in the world of 1000 B.C., those of India, Persia, China, Israel and the Mediterranean societies.

In India we find the primordial prophecy of Prajapathi, the Supreme Spirit taking on human flesh and offering himself up for the redemption of humanity. The *Rig Veda* of India (circa. 2000 B.C.), the most ancient and authoritative of the Hindu holy books, has a prophecy of the sacrifice of the mysterious Prajapathi ("Savior of man"), a being who is both divine and human. As laid out in the Vedic texts, the sacrifice of the God-man Prajapathi was performed by the kings and the priests. It is a sacrifice that is required for the redemption of humanity and only those who accept Prajapathi will be redeemed. These texts lay out the procedures for the sacrifice of Prajapathi[3]:

"His hands and legs are to be bound to a yoopa (a wooden pole) causing blood shed" (*Brihadaranyaka Upanishad 3.9.28. Ithareya Brahmanam 2:6.*)
"The sacrificial victim is to be crowned with a crown made of thorny vines" (*Rigveda* X: 90: 7,15) (*Bruhadaranyakopanishad* III:9:28)
"None of His bones must be broken." (*Yajurveda* XXXI. *Ithareya Brahmanam* 2.6).

"After death, His clothes are to be divided among the officers" (*Ithareya Brahmanam*)
"Before death he should be given a drink of somarasa [sour wine made of an herb called somalatha]. (*Yajur Veda* 31. *Ithareya Brahmanam*)

This prophesied sacrifice of Prajapathi underlies the sacrificial ceremonies prescribed in the holiest books of the Hindus, the Vedas.

In Persia too there is a prophesy of a final Savior who will judge the world and bring about the resurrection of the dead. Sacrifice is central to the Avesta, the holy book of the Persians. The haoma plant, which represents God become man, is offered as a sacrifice and the juice which results from the ritual confers immortality on those who partake of it.

In China, for some four thousand years it was believed that sacrifice to God (understood monotheistically) was required to maintain the cosmic order, what the Chinese called the Mandate of Heaven. The most important sacrifice was the Border Sacrifice which had to be performed annually by the Emperor himself in a solemn series of ceremonies that mirrored the Levitical rituals of the ancient Jews (for instance, the sacrificial victim had to be an unblemished first-born animal). Chan Kei Thong points out that "Access to God is obtained by the shedding of blood (at the altar), after which the emperor can enjoy communion with God at the meal (the table)."[4]

Sacrifice was tied to the Chinese idea of a covenant with Heaven just as in Israel. In fact, "the Chinese word translated as "covenant" is (xue meng), which literally means "blood covenant." Thong points out that "Both the Hebrew and Chinese historical records reveal a belief in the necessity of the death of a perfect sacrifice to cover the sins of the nation."[5]

Interestingly, Chinese court records describe an eclipse that took place at the time of the actual death of Christ (since the Chinese capital was five hours to the east of Jerusalem, it was experienced as a solar and a lunar eclipse): "In the day of Gui Hai, the last day of the month, there was a solar eclipse. [The emperor] avoided the Throne Room, suspended all military activities, and did not handle official business for five days. And he proclaimed, 'My poor character has caused this calamity, that the sun and the moon were veiled. I am fearful and trembling'" Another imperial edict about the same event reads, "'Yin and Yang have mistakenly switched, and the sun and moon were eclipsed. The sins of all the people are now on one man. [The emperor] proclaims pardon to all under heaven." The most extraordinary of all the interpretations of that two-thousand year-old event was this commentary in the Record of the Latter Han Dynasty, "Eclipse on the day of Gui Hai, Man from heaven died."[6]

As for the Mediterranean societies, the noted authority on antiquity Walter Burkert points out that, "Animal sacrifice was an all-pervasive reality in the ancient world. ... It is astounding, details aside, to observe the similarity of action and experience from Athens to Jerusalem and on to Babylon."[7]

In some ancient peoples, the initial impetus of atonement, purification and union with the Divine (seen as the Supreme Spirit) devolved into savagery and horrendous evil. But in the teachings and practices of the most ancient organized religions – in India, China, Persia and Israel – there is a commonality of theme that is astonishing. Distortions there were but underneath it all there is a constant focus on turning to the Most High and a sense of urgency about maintaining the cosmic order through sacrifice.

Also, as in India and Persia, there was a persistent idea in ancient Mediterranean and Near East societies of incarnate gods who died.

So here is a quiz: Which religion or people:

a. says that only a divine sacrifice will suffice for the atonement of the sins of humanity?
b. adds that this sacrifice for the redemption of humanity will require that: the victim be placed on a wooden pole; his hands and legs be pierced but no bones broken; a creeper with thorns be placed on his head; a drink of sour liquid be given to him; his clothes be divided among the offerors
c. claims that the savior of humanity will dispense final judgment, bring about the resurrection of the dead and inaugurate a new world
d. believes that a "scapegoat" will take on the sins of the people
e. reports a solar eclipse at the time of the death of Jesus and says "The man from heaven just died"

The answers may surprise you. (a) and (b) are found in the holiest books of Hinduism. (c) is from the religion of Persia that once dominated the world (d) is from ancient Greece (e) is from China.

If indeed there is a divine direction to human history, then the universal urge to sacrifice as well as the idea of a dying incarnate god can be seen as preparations for an event that affects all of history and all humanity. This is why it can be said that the religious history of humanity shows a pattern that comes to a climax in the life of Jesus of Nazareth.

To sum up, the primordial peoples, the hunter-gatherers who preceded all the organized religions and belief systems, believed in a supreme God whom they called Father and to whom they turned for all their needs. They were also driven by the need to perform sacrifice in expiation and propitiation.

When we come to the first systematically organized religions, those of the Indians, Chinese and Persians, every one of them, in their own distinctive ways, were alerted to a future event of great importance centered on sacrifice and atonement and salvation:

- the sacrifice of Prajapathi and the redemption of humanity;
- the Border Sacrifice to Shang Di in China and the astral occurrences that seem to have accompanied the birth and death of Jesus;
- the sacrifice of hoama and the prophecy of the Saoshyans in Persia.

The Mediterranean mystery religions were all about sacrifice and the incarnation of deity. And, finally, we have the Jewish nation who embodied in their own history the reality of sin and salvation, sacrifice and atonement, divine visitation and the promise of resurrection.

A.D.

All of this suggests that Jesus ("Savior") is the fulfillment not simply of the Jewish "idea" but of the beliefs and aspirations of the Indians, Chinese and Persians, of the primordial tribes and the Mediterranean mystery religions. Salvation is liberation from sin and its consequences, i.e., atonement, and this requires sacrifice and ultimately a perfect sacrifice: this is the thought pattern of humanity and it also happens to be the life pattern of Jesus. Moreover, it was not simply his life and teaching that is directly relevant to the religious history before him but also his death and resurrection and the new Life in God he proclaimed.

The momentum behind these movements of the human psyche is a fundamental insight into the nature of sacrifice and salvation and the awareness of a loving God who desires union with all his children. It is in this light that we can think of a rendezvous in world-history such that the religious history of humanity comes to a climax in the Jesus phenomenon. From all corners of the ancient world, China, Persia, India, Mesopotamia, Egypt, Africa, Mesoamerica, Australia, Palestine, we have a pincer movement of thought and practice that culminates in the proclamation: "You are to name him Jesus, because he will save his people from their sins."

Just as the cosmic movement of quantum fields and galaxies, stars and planets, chemicals and organisms finally culminated in the human self, so also the primordial pilgrimage of every major race and religion to their Creator and Savior reached its zenith in the revelation that here and now "God is with us": Emmanuel!

If Jesus was part of the divine plan of incarnation and salvation, then it would seem that the minds and hearts of the human race would be prepared for his coming. All the evidence available indicates that the psyche and intellect of humanity in the first century AD was attuned to the coming of Jesus.

We consider, in particular, the Jewish saga. The history of Israel, the prophecies of the holy messengers of God and the covenantal saga of God and his people suddenly seems to enter an irrevocable new horizon with the appearance of Jesus of Nazareth who is presented as the Davidic King of the Jews and Messiah of Israel. In him, with him and through him, all the great prophecies, premonitions and promises of the past were said to be fulfilled and the covenant itself came to a climax. This Jesus identified himself with the God of Israel claiming the authority to forgive sins, cleanse God's temple and determine the eternal destiny of every human person. His words, he said, would last beyond the passing of heaven and earth and his authority was greater than that of the Old Testament. He was Lord of the Sabbath, the personal embodiment of the Torah, a king with an everlasting kingdom and the ultimate judge of all.

A big picture emerges here: Jesus is indeed whom he said he was and whom his followers proclaimed him to be: the human locus of the divine: Son of God and Son of Man: God incarnate.

On a natural level, Jesus' coming could not have been better "timed." The spread of Christianity was made possible because of numerous factors: the laws instituted by the Romans (Pax Romana) and the roads they built across their far-flung empire; the philosophical treasury bequeathed by the Greeks (deployed in the doctrinal definitions of Christianity) along with the emergence of Greek as a universal language and culture thanks to Alexander the Great (hence the rapid distribution of Greek versions of the New Testament); the theological "purification" of the Jews in terms of monotheism and temple worship; and the ideas of incarnation, sacrifice, and atonement in the major world religions and mythologies. Moreover, the conceptual matrix of monotheism, incarnation, and divine law made possible the birth of modern science (which, in its turn, played a major role in the spread of Christianity). Each one of these developments was essential to the dissemination and assimilation of the Christian message. If God were to take on a human nature it would have to be at some point in history, and it can certainly be argued that if God was incarnate in Jesus the timing was optimal. It should be noted also that 98 percent of all the humans who ever lived have lived after the era of Jesus.

This would mean, of course, that nothing in religious history is a coincidence, nothing is an isolated atomic fact, nothing is unrelated to the phenomenon that is Jesus. The ideas that emerged in the heart of *Homo religiosus*, the ideas of the need for sacrifice and a savior, of a nameless tragedy where a god perished, of salvation and expiation and redemption, of some kind of afterlife that is related to one's deeds, were neither random events nor illusions of the imagination. This is not to say that God "planned" the evil that men do or the savagery and perversion of many of the religious beliefs and practices of *Homo sapiens* across millennia. Rather we are given a story of human choice on the one and the divine response on the other. It is also a story of a God who plants seeds of light even in the darkest hearts. It is a story of sin and its consequences – punishment, destruction, reparation. It is a story of a Lover who wishes to save, the Father, the Heart that is God, and of a humanity that desperately desires salvation in the midst of darkness and despair.

The Fullness of Time
Proclaiming God 2.0

The human understanding of God 1.0 reached its zenith in the revelation received by the people of Israel. This revelation told us that God was all-holy and self-existent (meaning he existed without beginning or end); that the world was his creation; that the evil and suffering in the world was a direct result of the sinful actions of humanity; and that some of the consequences of sin could be mitigated through acts of reparation and obedience to the divine law. The Old Testament portrays divinely ordained punishments for sin. But it also shows God pleading with his people to turn from idolatry and immorality, from sin and spiritual death.

Of course, the revelation came through human persons with their imperfections and limitations. But this groundwork was essential to set the stage for the climax to come. A revelation of God's inner being directly from God. God as Heart. God 2.0.

This final revelation came from God incarnate – from a divine Person who took on a human nature. Jesus the human face of God. Jesus the Word of God made flesh. Jesus the human smartphone with a divine SIM card.

At the appointed hour, "when the fullness of time had come, God sent his Son, born of a woman." (*Galatians* 4:4). Thus began the saga of God 2.0.

The Father Sends Us His Son and His Holy Spirit – the New Testament

God 2.0 is the story of a Father's Love for his children told by his Son through the Holy Spirit who is the ever-living Love of Father and Son. The New Testament chronicles our interaction with our Father, his Son and his Spirit. It is an interaction of hearts, human and divine.

A review of the relevant texts makes this clear.

The Father

We have said that, as a rule, Jesus personally addresses God as Father. At the same time, when talking of divine revelation and its application, Jesus does refer to God as "God" or "Lord" or "Most High." Take these instances:

- "They replied, "Caesar's." At that he said to them, "Then repay to Caesar what belongs to Caesar and to God what belongs to God." (*Matthew* 22:21)"
- "Concerning the resurrection of the dead, have you not read what was said to you by God, I am the God of Abraham, the God of Isaac, and the God of Jacob? He is not the God of the dead but of the living." (*Matthew* 22:31-2)
- "At this, Jesus said to him, "Get away, Satan! It is written: 'The Lord, your God, shall you worship and him alone shall you serve.'" (*Matthew* 4:10)

But when directly invoking God (with the exception of the Psalm 22 citation) or describing his relationship with God, he only uses the term "Father".

Jesus refers to God as Father over 160 times. By contrast, the entire Old Testament refers to God as Father only some 20 times – and mostly as a title.

It is also clear that the Father of whom Jesus speaks is the Lord of Heaven and Earth: "I give praise to you, Father, *Lord of heaven and earth.*" (*Matthew* 11:25)

Jesus' revelation of the Father unveils a tripod of truths disclosing a relationship within God and a relationship between God and us:

- *Fatherhood is intrinsic to the Godhead – we cannot think of God without thinking of his being Father* as consistently expounded by Jesus. Jesus' followers recognized this revelation in its fullness so that Paul's epistles talk of God the Father some forty times. The Aramaic word *Abba* is used in his epistles to Greek-speaking Gentiles to emphasize the intimacy of the fatherhood revealed by Jesus.
- At the same time, *Jesus makes it clear that God is Jesus' own Father in a way that is different from his being our Father*. This is obvious in the Gospels where Jesus distinguishes between *my* Father and *your* Father:
  - "Just so, your light must shine before others, that they may see your good deeds and glorify *your* heavenly Father." (*Matthew* 5:16)
  - "That you may be children of *your* heavenly Father." (*Matthew* 5:45)
  - "Take care not to perform righteous deeds in order that people may see them otherwise, you will have no recompense from *your* heavenly Father." (*Matthew* 6:1)
  - "And *your* Father who sees in secret will repay you." (*Matthew* 6:4)

- "Not everyone who says to me, 'Lord, Lord,' will enter the kingdom of heaven, but only the one who does the will of *my* Father in heaven." (*Matthew* 7:21)
- "Everyone who acknowledges me before others I will acknowledge before *my* heavenly Father." (*Matthew* 10:32)
- "Be merciful, just as [also] your Father is merciful." (*Luke* 6:36)
- "But go to my brothers and tell them, 'I am going to *my* Father and *your* Father, to *my* God and *your* God.'" (*John* 20:17)
- Jesus teaches the "Our Father" as a prayer that we are to use in praying to "our" Father.

This distinction between our relationship to the Father and Jesus' own relationship with his Father is emphasized also in the epistles: "God and Father of our Lord Jesus Christ." (*Romans* 15:6)

- *Jesus' relationship with the Father is qualitatively different from ours because his Sonship is intrinsic to the Godhead: the Father is Father because he has a Son and this Son is the Father's "spitting image!"*
  - "Whoever has seen me has seen the Father." (*John* 14:9)
  - "The Father and I are one." (*John* 10:30)

We cannot access the Father except through the Son. Further, as we will see, there is a third relationship "within" the Godhead, that of the Spirit sent by the Father through the Son.

The Son

Jesus' revelation was possible because of his unique knowledge of the Father and the nature of their relationship:

> "All things have been handed over to me by my Father. No one knows the Son except the Father, and no one knows the Father except the Son and anyone to whom the Son wishes to reveal him." (*Matthew* 11:27)

> "Jesus said to him, 'I am the way and the truth and the life. No one comes to the Father except through me.'" (*John* 14:6)

> "The words that I speak to you I do not speak on my own. The Father who dwells in me is doing his works. Believe me that I am in the Father and the Father is in me." (*John* 14:10)

Without Jesus there would be no revelation of the Father. Without Jesus, there would be no enduring relationship for us with the Father. In fact, Jesus' revelation of the Father was equally a revelation of his Sonship. So who was he?

Jesus said he was the Son of the Father specifically in the sense of sharing the same divine existence.

His enemies immediately grasped the connection. "The Jews tried all the more to kill him, because he not only broke the sabbath but he also called God his own father, making himself equal to God." (*John* 5:18)

To be the "only" Son of the Father is to possess the same "nature" as the Father. The Father is divine and therefore so is the Son. This is the proclamation of the New Testament.

As attested by the first accounts of Jesus' life, the recorded acts of his apostles and the proclamation of his church, more was claimed about him than of any other human being before or after. The claim was that Jesus is God incarnate, God and man, Eternity "time-stamped."

Jesus' resurrection, his miracles, his life of perfect holiness, his transcendent teaching, his changing of the laws of human existence testify to the truth of his divine status. We consider the framework of fact pointing to this startling reality in the next chapter.

Son of the Father

To recap: everything about Jesus centers on the Father:
> where he comes from,
>> his mission (sent by the Father to save the world),
>>> his identity as Son.

It is taken for granted that the Father is divine since the New Testament term for "God" (*ho theos*), in fact, is synonymous with "Father." Jesus says, "No one comes to the Father except through me." Moreover, "Whoever has seen me has seen the Father." And "The Father and I are one." The Father is God. The Son is God. And so complete is their union that they are One. To know the Son is to know the Father. The curtain is drawn further back when the Father directly manifests himself as Father at the baptism of Jesus: "This is my beloved Son, with whom I am well pleased." (*Matthew* 3:17).

The Holy Spirit

This celestial announcement is preceded by an equally dramatic event: John the Baptist "saw the Spirit of God descending like a dove [and] coming upon him [Jesus]." (*Matthew* 3:16). Immediately after the baptism, "*Filled with the holy Spirit*, Jesus returned from the Jordan and was *led by the Spirit* into the desert." (*Luke* 4:1). After the temptation in the desert, "Jesus returned to Galilee *in the power of the Spirit*." (*Luke* 4:14).

The Spirit was, in fact, active in the very conception of Jesus: "his mother Mary was ... found with child *through the holy Spirit*." (*Matthew* 1:18). Strikingly,

Jesus says: "Blasphemy against the Spirit will not be forgiven ... whoever speaks against the holy Spirit will not be forgiven." (*Matthew* 12:32). Also: "no one can enter the kingdom of God without being born of water and Spirit." (*John* 3:5).

In his final discourse, he tells the disciples: "I will ask the Father, and he will give you another Advocate to be with you always, The Spirit of truth, which the world cannot accept ... But you know it, because it remains with you, and will be in you." (*John* 14:16-17). "When the Advocate comes whom I will send you from the Father, the Spirit of truth that proceeds from the Father, *he will testify to me.*" (*John* 15:26). There is a condition: "If I do not go, the Advocate will not come to you. But if I go, I will send him to you." (*John* 16:7).

Spirit OF God

It is evident too that the Holy Spirit is divine for he is the Spirit *OF* God: distinct from Father and Son but acting with divine power. Jesus teaches that blasphemy against the Holy Spirit will not be forgiven in this world or the next. This is precisely because the Spirit is divine. And yet the Spirit is One with Father and Son. He is the Spirit of both Father and Son: "The Spirit of truth that proceeds from the Father," the ultimate Source, but also the "Spirit of his Son" through whom he proceeds. Like the Father, the Holy Spirit is also shown addressing the faithful: "While they were worshiping the Lord and fasting, the holy Spirit said, 'Set apart for me Barnabas and Saul for the work to which I have called them.'" (*Acts* 13:2).

Three-in-One

This revelation of the Trinity, the Three-in-One Reality of God, begins with the first major salvific event in the Gospels, the Annunciation:

> The archangel proclaims: "He will be great and he will be called the Son of the Most High...The Holy Spirit will come upon you, and the power of the most High will overshadow you; therefore the child to be born will be called holy, the Son of God." (*Luke* 1:32, 35).

The Three divine Persons within the One Godhead are identified.

The revelation of the Trinity reaches its climax in Jesus' last command in the Gospels:

> Baptize all peoples "in the name of the Father, and of the Son, and of the holy Spirit." (*Matthew* 28:19).

The Three-in-One matrix pervades the epistles:

> "The grace of the Lord Jesus Christ and the love of God and the fellowship of the holy Spirit be with you." (2 *Corinthians* 13:13).

At the level of proclamation and act, Jesus and the New Testament confirmed the universal intuition of the pre-Christian religions that God is Trinity: there is only one God and *within* that one God there are Three inter-penetrating, indwelling "centers": the Father, his Son and his Holy Spirit. This truth will be explored further as we proceed.

The Father as Source of the Son and the Holy Spirit

Here we should note that the Father is the eternal Source-less Source of the Son and the Spirit.

Doctors of the Trinity like Thomas Aquinas[1] have emphasized this fact that the Father is the "source" or "fount of the divinity" in the Trinity. Louis Bouyer observes that "Revelation is quite clear on this point: Christian monotheism is neither solely nor primarily that of a divine essence. It is that of the divine monarchy, of the Father, the one principle of divinity as of all that has come from it."[2]

The Churches of East and West agree on this as highlighted by the Pontifical Council for Promoting Christian Unity: "The Father alone is the principle without principle of the two other persons of the Trinity, the sole source of the Son and of the Holy Spirit. ... The two traditions recognize that the "monarchy of the Father" implies that the Father is the sole Trinitarian Cause or Principle of the Son and the Holy Spirit."[3]

Yet the Father cannot be considered other than in relation to Son and Spirit. The three Persons *are constituted by their mutual relationships*: the Father is Generator, the Son the image of the Father, the Holy Spirit the Gift that Father and Son present to each other.

The mutual relationships of the Three Persons are described by reference to their "origin": the Father is unbegotten, the Son is begotten from the Father, the Holy Spirit is neither unbegotten nor begotten but "proceeds" from the Father through the Son.

The relations of origin have no bearing on priority in time or equality. All Three entirely, equally, eternally possess the divine being. The Father gives all he is to the Son, the Son receives all he is from the Father, their common love "breathes" forth the Spirit.

"I am in the Father and the Father is in me." (*John* 14:11). "The Advocate ... whom I will send you from the Father, the Spirit of truth that proceeds from the Father." (*John* 15:26).

"They are each in each and all in each, and each in all and all in all, and all are one."[4]

The Father Revealed by Jesus

"But the hour is coming, and is now here, when true worshipers will worship the Father in Spirit and truth; and indeed the Father seeks such people to worship him." John 4:23

God is to be approached as Father.

True worship of God is worship of the Father.

The Father seeks out those who worship him in Spirit and truth.

This is the God revealed by Jesus of Nazareth.

God 2.0.

Jesus also tells us the kind of father God is:

- Prodigal – extravagant and lavish in his generosity and mercy
- *Abba* Father – intimately personal beyond any earthly parent and infinitely loving
- Our Father – a Father to be approached for every one of our needs and goals

We will consider each of these characteristics in a later chapter.

The Father and the "Structure" of God

But in speaking of God as Father, Jesus also made it clear that this is one dimension of the "structure" or "being" of God. There were three dimensions of the Godhead that needed to be revealed: the inner being of God, the "outer" being of God, and the being of God as it relates to us. Jesus made unprecedented revelations about each of these dimensions.

R.A. Varghese

The Three Dimensions of the Being of God

He revealed:

- *The "outer" being of the Godhead* – God is Spirit: God is infinite-eternal and beyond all physical and other limitations.
- *The "inner" being of the Godhead* – God is Trinity: God is infinite interpersonal Love, Three Divine Persons with One Mind and Will united in a never-ending State of in-love-ness.
- *The Godhead **in relation to us*** – God as *Abba*: God is our infinitely loving Father who adopts us as his children in his divine Son through his divine Spirit.

Often, however, "infinite Spirit" and "Trinity" turn into meaningless abstractions.

We overcome this problem when we recognize God as literally an infinite-eternal Love Story. It is a story that has no beginning or end. The infinite-eternal Father's infinite Love eternally generates his Son and their infinite Love bears fruit in the eternal Gift known as the Holy Spirit. Three "centers" in a single Ultimate Reality of Love. One Heart.

To "relate" to God, we have to start with Abba, our infinitely loving Father.

It is the Father's infinite Love for us, his Paternal Heart, that is responsible for his sending us his Son and his Spirit:

> "For God so loved the world that he gave his only Son, so that everyone who believes in him might not perish but might have eternal life." (*John* 3:16)

> "For those who are led by the Spirit of God are children of God. ... You received a spirit of adoption, through which we cry, "Abba, Father!" (*Romans* 8:14-15)

When we pray, we pray to the Father in the name of the Son ("whatever you ask in my name, I will do" *John* 14:13) by the power of the Spirit.

Clearly, the existence of God as infinite Spirit, his Triune Being and the Incarnation of the Son are fundamental to the revelation of Jesus. While we will consider all of these breakthroughs in turn, our primary mission is to "recover" the Father.

And so we return to the Father.

Abba as Fundamental to Understanding and Interacting with God

Abba is the Aramaic word for personally addressing one's own father. It suggests intimacy and affection. Jesus' use of *Abba* in talking to and about God and his emphasis on God as Father tells us one thing. It indicates that *Abba* is fundamental to our understanding of God and our relationship with him.

Here is what we see in the New Testament:

- Throughout the Gospels, Jesus only addresses God as "Father" with the single exception of his cry from the cross where he is quoting from Psalm 22.
- The Aramaic word *Abba* is highlighted in the Greek text of the New Testament, once in the Gospels, twice in the Epistles, because
    - it derives directly from Jesus: such a radically new usage would have to originate in him.
    - the Greek "pater" does not capture the intimacy of *Abba*, an intimacy revealed by Jesus.

Jesus' referring to God as *Abba* is remarkable, among other things, because *it is unique in religious literature*. Jean Galot points out that this personalized invocation of God as *Abba* was unheard-of in Jewish religious language given the Jewish emphasis on God's transcendence.

Certainly, Jews of Jesus' time and before have spoken of God as the Father of Israel. The famous Avinu Malkeinu prayer is addressed to "Our Father, Our King" drawing on *Isaiah* 63:16 and 33:22.

But, as Jewish scholar Alon Goshen-Gottstein points out[5], the Jewish reference to God as Father has primarily been metaphorical and it is more in the nature of a title like "King." God is Father as life-giver and law-giver. In contrast, in the case of Jesus and later of his followers, as Goshen-Gottstein notes, the Father is *experienced as personally present and active*.

At the same time, we should remember that, from the beginning, the human race has had an instinctive understanding of God as Father. It was inevitably incomplete but nevertheless touching.

We quoted anthropologist Walter Schmidt who investigated Stone Age cultures: "The name 'father" is applied to the Supreme Being in every single area of the primitive culture when he is addressed or appealed to." Schmidt adds that "There is no doubt possible that the name 'father' is intended in this connexion to denote, not physiological paternity ..., but an attitude of the greatest reverence, of tender affection, and steadfast trust on the part of man towards his god."[6]

In African religion too, God is often seen as Father, says Aloysius Lugira: "A number of African people look to God as Father and themselves as his children. This image gives the idea of a family. It shows a close relationship between people and God. It implies that God has not only 'begotten' or made the people, but is also their protector, provider and keeper. ... The idea of God as Father or Parent is also shown in prayers which people offer to him. The prayers are addressed to him in a manner similar to that of children speaking to their parents about themselves and their needs."[7] The ancient Middle Eastern societies likewise saw God as the supreme "all-father."

This ancient intuitive sense of God as Father is consolidated and amplified in the revelation of Jesus who calls him *Abba* Father. About this usage, the New Testament scholar James D.G. Dunn writes: *"The evidence points consistently and clearly to the conclusion that Jesus' regular use of 'abba' in addressing God distinguished Jesus in a significant degree from his contemporaries. ...* We know abba primarily as a word belonging to the family and expressive often of intimate family relationship – hence presumably its unfitness for the solemnity of prayer in the view of almost all Jesus' contemporaries. ... Jesus' use of it was not merely a formal convention, but expressed *a sense of sonship,* indeed ... of intimate sonship."[8]

Yes, *Abba* is an intimate form of addressing our fathers. As it applies to God, we should remember that any finite idea applied to God has to be thought off as infinitely applicable. If we say God is good, we have to think of him as infinitely good. If God is thought off with the same intimacy as we think of our fathers whether as a child or an adult, in either case he has to be thought of as being infinitely more intimate than our earthly fathers. "Daddy" is not intimate enough!

Jesus himself made this very point as it applied to children and their fathers: "What father among you would hand his son a snake when he asks for a fish? Or hand him a scorpion when he asks for an egg? If you then, who are wicked, know how to give good gifts to your children, how much more will the Father in heaven give the holy Spirit to those who ask him?" (*Luke* 11:11-3).

Can We Call God "Abba"?

Yes, Jesus calls his Father "Abba". But can we do this as well? The New Testament tells us that only those who have received the Spirit of God through Jesus are able to call God "Abba."

Abba is used three times in the New Testament. The first is when, in *Mark*, Jesus speaks to the Father at Gethsemane. The two other instances are in *Romans* and *Galatians*. In these two latter cases, we are told that the Father sends the Spirit into the hearts of those redeemed by Jesus who then cry out "Abba Father."

Dunn remarks that "The clear implication of Rom. 8.15f. and Gal. 4.6f is that Paul regarded the abba prayer as something distinctive to those who had received the eschatological Spirit." It was "a distinguishing mark of those who shared the Spirit of Jesus' sonship, of an inheritance shared with Christ."[9]

During his earthly ministry, only Jesus could address Father as *Abba* because of his relationship as the Only Son. But after his redemptive death, the coming of the Holy Spirit, and our adoption into Jesus through the Holy Spirit we too can call God our *Abba*. This is because those who accept Jesus' invitation have been redeemed by Jesus and are indwelt by the Holy Spirit. Thereby they become children of the Father in the fullest possible sense. We are hearts embedded in his Heart.

Who is Prodigal in the Parable?

It has been said that in the parable of the Prodigal Son, it is the father who is prodigal. This is because "prodigal" means extravagant and in the parable it is the father who is extravagant in his generosity.

In the parable, Jesus seeks to give us a portrait of the Heavenly Father who is infinitely generous. It is interesting to note that that, even at a human level, the father in the parable goes beyond common Jewish ideas of the role of the father.

Biblical scholar Richard Bauckham elaborates on the difference between the radical father in the parable and the father in patriarchal societies:

> The head of a household was supposed to be a dignified figure of authority, used to people doing as he said. This father probably surprises Jesus' audience from the word go, when, instead of putting his foot down and maintaining his right to his property until death, he lets the younger son have his way. ... The father would have surprised Jesus' audience again in a detail you might not have noticed: when he sees his son returning home, the father runs to meet him. In those days mature and dignified men, heads of households, did not run. We can see in that detail the overwhelming force of this father's love for his son. If he runs to meet his son, then one can hardly be surprised that he has no word of reproach or condemnation, nothing but totally unconditional welcome. For the third occasion on which the father fails to conform to the cultural model of the authoritarian patriarch we have to continue with the story to the point when the elder son refuses to join in the celebrations. He stays outside the house, and his father comes out and pleads with him. Fathers do not plead, they command. But this father pleads. He reflects the Father God who constantly surprises us with his patience, his compassion and his gentle, non-coercive love.[10]

Our Father

Although, as we have seen, the people of Israel did speak of God as Father, there was a decisive difference in Jesus' description of him as "our Father."

The Jewish scholar cited earlier, Alon Goshen-Gottstein, observes that "For Judaism, both ancient and later, 'Father' never ceases to be a metaphor. ... There is no absolute sense in which God is spoken of as Father."

The contrast with Jesus' teaching, says Goshen-Gottstein, is clear: "What is unique and special about Jesus is the measure in which what for others is simply a stock part of religious language was lived as a vivid, personal experience of God."

So much so that for followers of Jesus, "'Father' ceases to be metaphorical and is to be understood as revealing something substantive about God. ... In fact, one can say that "Father" becomes part of the very definition of God."[11]

Unlike in Judaism, in Jesus' revelation the Fatherhood of God is fundamental to the very being of God. It tells us what God is like in his infinite-eternal reality. It tells us that there is a communion of persons *within* God of which the Father is the Source. It is a communion of love, an affair of the Heart.

Unprecedented though it was, the revelation of Fatherhood *within* God was front and center in the teaching of Jesus. It was the key to his own mission and identity.

The Voice of the Father

But there was even more to come in terms of uniqueness.

Just as unimaginable, and startling beyond belief, is the Father's Voice from Heaven proclaiming Jesus to be "*my* beloved Son."

There is no comparable phenomenon in any major religion.

The Father himself manifests his Presence to the followers of the Son *as Father*!

Time Out
Exploring God 2.0

Dazzling as it was, the revelation of God 2.0 raised three puzzles:

> Its truth rested on the assumption that its revealer was God incarnate. But how can we know this to be case?
>
> By speaking of a human being as God incarnate are we guilty of idolatry or polytheism?
>
> What does it mean to say that there are three Persons "within" God?

The followers of Jesus were pre-occupied with these reasonable questions for some seven centuries. In wrestling with them, they produced a stunning and compelling portrait of God that not only changed human history but transformed human society.

Most importantly, Jesus' revelation of God as a Trinity of Persons gave birth to today's idea of the human person (as pointed out, for instance, by the logician Peter Geach). Unbelievably, the idea of a "person" that we take for granted never existed in any prior culture. It came to be because of the inquiry into the Trinity and today forms the foundation of human dignity and human rights. Likewise, it was the insight into the incarnation of God in Jesus that gave birth to modern science. The Incarnation helped us to recognize that the universe is separate from God and that it follows rational laws because it was created by an infinitely intelligent Mind (as highlighted by historians of science like Stanley Jaki).

Essential though they were, these centuries-long explorations into God 2.0 eclipsed Jesus' focus on the Father. In our present journey, we are seeking to retrieve and restore the freshness of the original revelation. But this is not an either/or situation. We can better understand what was meant by Jesus in the light of the seven-century exploration of the matrix of God 2.0. So now let us taste and see the fruits of this exploration.

We will begin with Jesus' revelation that God is spirit which is essential for our understanding of God as infinite. In fact, it is essential for monotheism. From there we will consider the basis for claiming that Jesus is God incarnate – and what this means. Finally, we will try to make what sense we can of the never-ending love story we call the Trinity.

Infinite Spirit

The world with its limitations could not exist if there was no Being that has the Power of always existing. A Being with no limitations (of knowledge, power. et al.). To say that this Being – God – has no limitations is to say that God is infinite. This would mean that God would have to be "spirit" in the sense of not being limited by space. (By "spirit" here we are not talking about the Holy Spirit but of the non-physical nature of God).

Along with his revelation of the Father, Jesus also revealed that God is Spirit: "God is Spirit, and those who worship him must worship in Spirit and truth.'" (*John* 4:24)

No one can understand either the Trinity or the Incarnation of the Son without grasping the radical truth that God is Spirit. In fact, true monotheism is impossible without this insight. A spirit has no parts and does not occupy space. It has an intellect and a will. An infinite Spirit is one that exercises the capabilities of intellect and will without limitation of any kind. *It was Jesus of Nazareth who revealed the necessarily spiritual nature of God.*

True monotheism was made possible only with the revelation that God is Spirit. Despite using the phrase "spirit of God," the Old Testament had yet to reach this insight and, in fact, the *Jewish Encyclopedia* explicitly denies the claim that God is Spirit: "The phrase "spirit of God" ("ruaḥ Elohim") merely describes the divine energy, and is not to be taken as equivalent to the phrase "God is a spirit," viz., an assertion concerning His incorporeality (Zech. iv. 6; Num. xiv. 22; Isa. xl. 13)."[1]

But only if God is spirit (not limited by matter) could he be infinite (without limitation). Thus, Jesus' revelation of God as spirit enables the New Testament proclamation that God is infinite, i.e., without limitation of any kind, and infinitely personal. Without this insight, other monotheisms have ended up with ideas of a finite god, a physical god, a changing god, an impersonal god or force – none of which are compatible with monotheism or even theism.

Make no mistake: we cannot be monotheists if we do not accept this fundamental revelation of Jesus.

To recap, spirit does not occupy space. It is not physical, i.e. quantifiable, and therefore not subject to scientific study. Spirit is present where it acts. We are finite spirits united with matter. The "I" that is "me" is not in any part of my brain or body. It cannot be detected with any device. It is present where it acts. Of course, in the case of humans, spirit is integrated with matter as a unified reality.

God, on the other hand, is infinite spirit, spirit without limitation of any kind. The two primary acts of spirit are knowing and willing (and love is an act of the will): knowing what is true, loving what is good. As we shall see, to say God is Trinity is to say that, as Spirit, God exists, knows and loves infinitely. The Trinity is the infinite Spirit in its existing, knowing and loving.

But on what basis can we accept Jesus' claim that God is spirit or Trinity?

How We Know That Jesus Is God Incarnate

The revelation of God 2.0 rests on the foundation of Jesus' identity as God incarnate. To say Jesus of Nazareth is God incarnate is to affirm that God manifested his Triune (Three-in-One) Being and Action in the existence of Jesus of Nazareth. Jesus was the locus of the divine in human terms. From start to finish, from conception, baptism and ministry to death, resurrection and ascension, Jesus' life was above all a manifestation of the tri-personal God: he was the Son, filled with the Holy Spirit, doing the Will of his Father. Every human person is made in the image of God. Jesus is a divine Person in the image of man: The Triune SIM card/network/power-source in the human smartphone.

Here is the cumulative case for the affirmation that Jesus is God incarnate:

1	**Claim to be God Incarnate**
	First and foremost, Jesus claimed to be God incarnate and his followers understood him to make this claim. This is why he was crucified, his followers persecuted. Jesus' divine claim was made in the terms understood by the Jews of his time: e.g., claiming to have the attributes proper to God such as forgiving sins; taking the divine Name ("I AM"); placing himself on the same level as the Torah, the Word of God, and the Temple, the dwelling-place of God. He was acclaimed as God united to a human nature by his followers right from the first century as is evident from their writings. Jesus is the only "founder" of a world religion to make this claim about himself. Minimally, only such a claim would make it worth our while to study a claim of divine revelation. This is because only God incarnate could authoritatively tell us the truth about God and ourselves. A prophet or sage who is solely and simply human can only speak as one who believes and not as one who knows. Only God incarnate can KNOW. Hence only the revelation of God incarnate has the seal of divine truth.

2. Resurrection from the Dead

Jesus was the only person of whom it is claimed: he rose from the dead and continues to be active in human life and history. The testimony of the transformed apostles and the entire church from its earliest days to the present is singular in its unanimity and consistency: the crucified Jesus physically rose from the dead. The most compelling feature of the claim of resurrection is the transformation of the followers of Jesus and the genesis of the Christian movement. What transformed eleven fearful peasants and fisher-folk into superheroes who preached the Good News across the world despite trials and tribulations and eventually horrendous deaths? What galvanized them to take on the most powerful empire of the day? The hallucination hypothesis is not remotely plausible for those who know the causes and characteristics of hallucinations (an individual experience, drugs, mental illness, an expectation of seeing that which is allegedly witnessed – none of which apply in the present case). The idea of a hoax is wildly implausible given the improbability that anyone would embrace a gruesome end in order to perpetrate a fiction. These kinds of counter-explanations remind us of what George Orwell once said, "One has to belong to the intelligentsia to believe things like that. No ordinary man could be such a fool." The Jewish rabbi Pinchas Lapide, who accepted the Resurrection, said "When these peasants, shepherds, and fishermen, who betrayed and denied their master and then failed him miserably, suddenly could be changed overnight into a confident mission society, convinced of salvation and able to work with much more success after Easter than before Easter, then no vision or hallucination is sufficient to explain such a revolutionary transformation."[1] It seems undeniable that the extraordinary transformation could only be explained by an extraordinary event and, in this respect, the Resurrection makes perfect sense. The most influential philosopher of the 20th century, Ludwig Wittgenstein (also Jewish), believed in the Resurrection and said "What inclines even me to believe in Christ's resurrection? ... If I am to be REALLY saved, - what I need is CERTAINTY - not wisdom, dreams or speculations - and this certainty is faith."[2]

3	**Unique Phenomenon**

It is a matter of historical hard fact that a unique phenomenon emerged in the first century A.D.: the calendaring system of human history itself was transformed into B.C and A.D., i.e., "before" and "after" the genesis of this phenomenon. What we see is a story, a proclamation, a testimony, a call to thought and action that creates a new kind of community. It is a community with its own structure, its own rules and rituals, its raison d'etre. And it is a community that is centered on the life and message, the death and resurrection and the divine identity of a singular individual. Jesus was not simply embedded in the very life of the community but the community believed itself to embody Jesus. They spoke with his authority and acted on his behalf. An astonishing ensemble of evidence bears witness to this phenomenon: documents on the life of Jesus that precede the sacking of Jerusalem in 70 A.D., churches in Rome active by the middle of the first century, liturgies focused on the passion, death and resurrection of Christ with roots in the ancient Jewish worship rituals, creeds and initiation procedures taught during the Roman persecution, teachings from church authorities dating back to the first century, ancient Christian communities started by followers of Jesus that teach the "Gospel truth", writings by Church Fathers going back to the first century.

4	**One-on-one Encounter**

Jesus is the only person about whom his followers say that they know him from personal encounter in the present. Nothing similar has even been claimed about any transformational figure in world history starting with their appearance on the public stage. Right from the beginning, Jesus was believed to have been "present" to his followers and this one-on-one encounter has continued over the centuries and in the lived experience of hundreds of millions of people. Take, for instance, the revivalist who claims to personally experience the presence of the Savior or a Mother Teresa who saw Jesus in the poor or the believer who hears Jesus speak to her directly through the Gospels or the missionary in a remote jungle who feels the hand of the Lord in the face of travails and turmoil. They claim to be *acted on* by a reality external to them and by its very nature such an encounter is self-authenticating and not something susceptible to external criteria. For those who have experienced the encounter, the claim is a rational response to their experience (whether or not an outsider takes the claim at face value). This is not a leap in the dark but a leap to the light. This claim was made from the very beginning of the phenomenon of Jesus and has been historically continuous with its growth. In that respect there is nothing similar in history.

5	**Miracles and the Miraculous**
	Non-Christian historians admit that the historical Jesus, at the very least, worked miracles (or was believed to do so). The miracles attributed to Jesus in the Gospels were not performed to amaze or impress. They were acts of compassion in response to tearful requests. He was no wonder-worker. He was a healer and provider. He gave sight and speech. He cured the lame, the paralyzed, and the leprous. He brought the dead to life. He gave food to the hungry. He did what an infinite lover would do. Moreover, the spread of Christianity was always accompanied by claims of the miraculous. The miracle stories of the Gospels are paralleled by miracle traditions associated with the ministries of all the apostles. And this has been followed by a tidal wave of claims of miracles of every kind. Scholars face the temptation of living entirely in the world of the text. They tend not to realize that the events reported in the text pertain to the real world—let alone to the supernatural realm. Theirs is a different mindset from that of either the primordial Christians or the believers of today: the devout are in touch with the world of the supernatural, and many report a response from the other side. If there is indeed a supernatural impetus behind the worldwide dissemination of the message of Jesus, this would comport well with the claims made about him by his followers. One would almost expect such an impetus.
6	**Savior**
	The problem is that we are sinful—and we need to be saved from our sins. This is a matter of history not theology: the universal awareness of a breach between humanity and the Divine made sacrifice in atonement THE primordial practice of the human race. The problem is that our sin is against God—it is a sin that has led to the current human condition: evil, suffering, death. To make atonement for this sin, to pay the price for this sin, the person who does so must be capable of doing so in terms of making an infinite reparation while also being human. And this reparation must be such as to make heaven possible for us, must cure the evil that is within us, must decisively allow us to go beyond death, must make happiness possible here and now. And all of this must take place in the course of human history because that is the matrix that determines human destiny. And it is all of this that the New Testament writers claimed about Jesus: "You are to name him Jesus, because he will save his people from their sins" (*Matthew* 1:21).

| 7 | **The Purpose of Life** |

If death is the end, then none of our actions on earth have any ultimate meaning or point. This is the problem that the philosophers and the sages could not resolve since they themselves were destined for oblivion. If Jesus was truly God incarnate, then we would expect him to not only acknowledge the problem but also to give us a solution. He did both, going right to the heart of the problem: "What profit is there for one to gain the whole world and forfeit his life? What could one give in exchange for his life?" (*Mark* 8:36–37). "For whoever wishes to save his life will lose it, but whoever loses his life for my sake and that of the gospel will save it." (*Mark* 8:35). "Then the king will say to those on his right, 'Come, you who are blessed by my Father. Inherit the kingdom prepared for you from the foundation of the world' … And these [the wicked] will go off to eternal punishment, but the righteous to eternal life." (*Matthew* 25:34, 46). His answer was the only viable one, the one that only God could give: we are called to live forever, and our choices in this life determine our everlasting destiny. To make the wrong choices is to lose it all. Everything matters. Everything is meaningful. Like there are laws of nature, there are laws of human existence: you will die and your life after death (as understood by the human race even before Christ) could well be a life of separation from God. But Jesus changed the laws of human existence: through him, you can live with the life of God and live forever with God: this is greater than changing than the laws of nature: it is changing the laws of human existence. This is redemption. This is the Good News.

| 8 | **The Life of God** |

Jesus did not simply speak of the life to come. He had come so that we "might have life and have it more abundantly" (John 10:10) – here and now. In coming as Savior, Jesus invited us all to be filled with the life of God, the Holy Spirit. "As proof that you are children, God sent the Spirit of his Son into our hearts, crying out, 'Abba, Father!'" (*Galatians* 4:6). Consequently, as the Apostle Paul put it, "We are the offspring of God." (*Acts* 17:39). Eternity begins here, now for "I live, no longer I, but Christ lives in me." (*Galatians* 2:20).

9	**The Rendezvous of the Religions. The Convergence of the World-historical Process.**
	We have seen that all the great pre-Christian religious movements and ideas and rituals—from India to Persia, China to Israel, Greece to Babylon—point to sacrifice and expiation, incarnation and salvation. These themes come to a climax in the life and teaching, the death and resurrection of Jesus. The story of his life and mission seemed to represent the climax and consummation of themes and aspirations articulated and developed in the fundamental matrix of the religions and mythologies that appeared before him. It is almost as if he historically embodied what was mythologically, thematically and prophetically encoded. Thus the story of Jesus and his sacrifice was neither isolated nor parochial. It was, you might say, a story that had already been written on the heart of humankind.
10	**Who is God?**
	Jesus irrevocably changed the human understanding of God. God is LOVE. The Incarnation of God in Christ is a manifestation to humanity of the inner Being of God. Through Jesus of Nazareth, we see God as Trinity: Three Divine Persons in one Divine Nature ("Triune"): Father, Son and Holy Spirit (neither "Father" nor "Son" should be understood biologically: these are metaphors pointing to an infinite-eternal relationship of giving and receiving). Everything in the existence of Jesus involved the action of the Three Persons. He was the Logos/Son made flesh. He was filled with the Holy Spirit. He was sent by the Father and to see him was to see the Father.
	"Trinity" is not God's proper name. It is simply a way of saying that God is infinite love. To say that God is Trinity is simply to say that God is LOVE.

So Is Jesus God Incarnate?

When connected, these ten data-points paint a big picture A vision emerges from the data, unifying it and making it coherent: that of a divine Person uniting himself to a human nature: Jesus of Nazareth. The Logos/Word/Son is divine. In the Incarnation, the Logos "acquires" a human body and soul. Thus we have a divine Person with both a divine nature and a human nature. In his divine nature, he is infinite. In his human nature, he is finite. Nevertheless, in his essential being, the Logos is infinite. But because the human nature is something he has "taken on," he is fully human. Fully human but not merely human.

It should be said that the question of the Incarnation of God in Christ is not a contemporary partisan Jewish-Christian dispute. According to the Pew research group, some 1.7 million adult American Jews now consider themselves Christian.[3] Many of them were secular or practicing Jews who came to this affirmation on their own. Some even saw the institutional church as antagonistic or alien. Nevertheless, they followed the evidence where it led them: to Jesus, the Messiah of Israel.

Paradoxically, the three greatest Jewish thinkers in modern history, Baruch Spinoza, Albert Einstein and Ludwig Wittgenstein, were fascinated by Christ. In his Tractatus Theologico-Politicus, Spinoza writes, "God manifested Himself to the Apostles through the mind of Christ as He formerly did to Moses through the supernatural voice. In this sense the voice of Christ, like the voice which Moses heard, may be called the voice of God, and it may be said that the wisdom of God (i.e. wisdom more than human) took upon itself in Christ human nature, and that Christ was the way of salvation."[4]

Affirmation of the Incarnation is logically sound. Michael Dummett, Wykeham Professor of Logic at Oxford University, says about this, "Should we then speak of a leap of faith at this point? I should rather speak of an act of judgment ... We know from the New Testament of Christ and of the actions of his Apostles, that the astonishing doctrine of the Incarnation is more credible than the rival hypotheses."[5]

The recognition of Jesus as God incarnate is not a matter of arguments or formulas. It is a perception not a thought: it is a coming to see. God's incarnation is revealed by God incarnate and this revelation is self-guaranteeing for those whose minds and hearts are open to discerning the action of the divine. Thus Marshall McLuhan, the prophet of the Internet, said recognition of the incarnation is a matter of perception not conception. It is "a percept because, as Christ said over and over again, it is visible to babes, but not to sophisticates."[6] But to see we have to open our eyes. As McLuhan put it, "If I hadn't believed it, I wouldn't have seen it."[7]

A Footnote – The "I" referred to by Jesus when he speaks of himself

Everyday experience tells us that when we say "I" about ourselves, we refer to the "I" with respect to one or other specific dimension of ourselves. When I say "I am made up of oxygen, carbon, hydrogen, nitrogen, calcium, phosphorus, potassium, sulfur, sodium, chlorine, and magnesium," I am speaking of the "I" with reference to my physical being. When I say "I am very good at math," I am speaking of the "I" with reference to my mental reality.

This is especially true about the way in which Jesus refers to himself because he is God incarnate, a divine Person taking on a human nature while also having a divine nature. Consequently, in reading the Gospels, we must distinguish between Jesus saying "I" in his human nature and "I" in his divine nature. The reference of the "I" is different depending on whether or not He speaks of it in his human or his divine nature. If he says "I am six feet tall," he is speaking with reference to the "I" in his human nature. When he says, "I forgive your sins," he is speaking with reference to the "I" in his divine nature. When he says the Son does not know "that hour or day," he is speaking with reference to the Son in his human nature. When he says, "Before Abraham was, I AM," he is speaking with reference to the "I" in his divine nature.

We now turn to the question of why we say that God is Trinity: Three Persons in One God.

Why We Say That God Is Trinity

The revelation of the Tri-Personal God is the breath-taking Truth that makes sense of all other truths. It is the luminous Mystery that illuminates all other mysteries. And it is the dazzling sun that allows us to see all things except itself – and this not because of darkness but its own excess of light. It is the revelation that makes sense of everything in our experience, EVERYTHING.

We can drill deeper into the mystery of the Trinity by addressing a few common questions:

- What We Can Know About the Trinity on a natural level?
- Is there any indication of the Trinity in the World Religions?
- How can you be Three and One?

The Infinite Perfection of God Requires Inter-Personal Love

The intuition that there is a relationship within God is present even at a natural level. Here is the rationale as laid out by Richard of St. Victor:

Since God is infinitely perfect, he must be infinite love, manifesting true and supreme love. But since love is personal and inter-personal, this would mean there has to be personal love within God. Such love at an infinite level is possible only if directed to one who is infinite.

Also, being perfect, God must have fullness of happiness and this is possible only from a mutual love that arises from giving and receiving. Thus, the self-donation required for true love calls for at least Two who are infinite, eternal and equal in one God.

But the Two would want a common object of their love, a communication of their love for each other that is itself Another: hence there would be Three co-equal "centers" within the One Godhead.

Daddy, We Never Knew You!

In short, since God is infinite, his loving, its object and its fruit must likewise be infinite: Lover, beloved, co-beloved. I, Thou, Ours. Father, Son, Holy Spirit: Three inseparable "centers" that ARE the One.

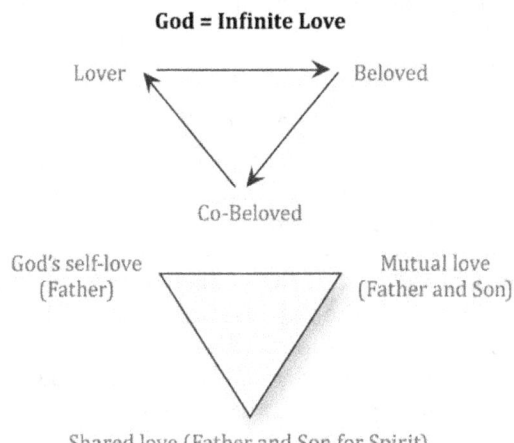

Now this is simply an intuition – but it is one which is expressed in the world religions and definitively confirmed by Jesus.

The Trinity in the World Religions

Turning to the religious history of humanity, we see that the divine Trinity seems pre-figured in the three main human approaches to God: the religious traditions of India, China, and Israel. These approaches are: historical-linear (Israel); cyclic-mystical (India); and unity-in-multiplicity/harmony (China).

In the Hindu holy books of India, God is called Saccidananda: Being, Knowledge, Bliss. Like other Hindu thinkers, Mahadev Govind Ranade (1842-1906) saw the connection between the Trinity and the Saccidananda description of the divine: "Sat.... the absolute existence of the Father, Chit ... the Logos, and Ananda ...the Holy Comforter."[13]

In China we have the ancient Taoist belief in God as the "Three Pure Ones." Taoist scholar Hsing-Tsung Huang notes the Chinese believed there were three centers in God[14]: These "Three Pure Ones" were seen as manifestations of the one Tao. The *Tao Te Ching* teaches: "The Tao produced One; One produced Two; Two produced Three; Three produced All things." The First Pure One : "The Universally Honored One of Origin" or "The Celestial Worthy of the Primordial Beginning." The Second Pure One: "The Celestial Worthy of the Numinous Treasure" who reveals the Taoist scriptures. The Third Pure One "The Celestial Worthy of the Way and its Power" or "The Universally Honored One of Tao and Virtues."

The Triune reality of GOD is prototyped in the Tanakh, the Hebrew Bible, and expounded in ancient Jewish writings. In the Old Testament, writes Gerard O'Collins, God is described as Father over 20 times, Word or Wisdom over 300 times, Spirit over 400 times. We have seen that God is called Elohim, a plural noun used in a singular sense, 2,570 times starting with *Genesis* 1. In fact, as we saw, God, his Word and his Spirit are specifically referenced in the *Genesis* account of creation.

Later in *Genesis* (18:1-2) we read: "The LORD appeared to Abraham by the oak of Mamre .., Looking up, he saw three men standing near him." Who are the Three who are referred to as Lord? Here, it is traditionally said, we have a "type" of the Trinity: a prefiguration and symbol.

The Jewish philosopher Philo (20 BC – 50 AD) said of this episode: "the one in the middle is the Father of the universe ... I am that I am; And the beings on each side are those most ancient powers ... one of which is called his creative power, and the other his royal power.And the creative power is God, for it is by this that he made and arranged the universe; And the royal power is the Lord, for it is fitting that the Creator should ... govern the creature ...

"Therefore the middle person ... presents to the mind ... a vision at one time of one being, and at another time of three."

Perhaps there is an intuition of the Triune in *Isaiah* (48:12): The divine Redeemer speaks: "Listen to me, Jacob ...I, it is I who am the first, and am I the last." He continues (48:16): "'Come near to me and hear this! ... 'Now the Lord GOD has sent me, and his spirit.' Church Fathers like Origen and Jerome saw this passage as stating: The Lord God has sent his Redeemer and his Spirit to his people.

Amazingly, two key words in the Shema, the greatest Jewish invocation of monotheism, make it compatible with the Triune reality of God. The Shema opens with *Deuteronomy* 6:4[8]: "Hear O Israel, the Lord our God, the Lord is One." Here the word used for God, "elohim," is a plural noun, and the word used for "one," "echad," is used often to describe a composite unity.

There is obviously no doctrine of the Trinity in the pre-Christian worlds. Rather, what we have are stories in search of an ending.

Three and One

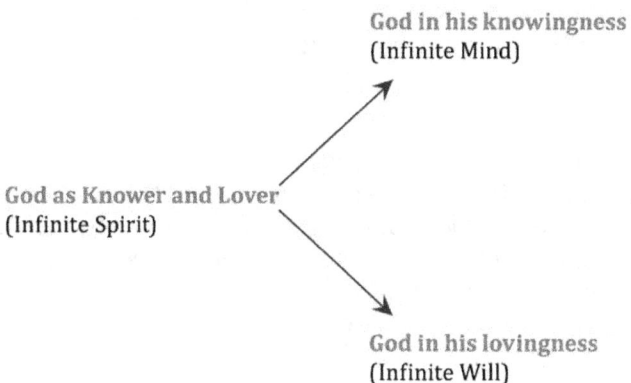

Father
The Godhead *exists eternally* without beginning or end as *the Source* and Summit of infinite perfection. This is the Father.

Son
The Godhead's *infinite act of knowing itself* performed with its infinite Mind *has to* be a perfect intellectual Image of itself. Why? The act of *knowing* is infinite; its *object* (the Godhead itself) has to be infinite; so the result of the knowing, the "image," has to be infinite.

This Image must contain EVERYTHING that is true of its Source, all its infinite perfection (other than being Source): This means it must itself be an infinite Person in its own right (the Logos/Thought/Word) with the same nature and power as its Source. This is the Son.

Holy Spirit
The Godhead's *infinite act of loving itself*, performed with its infinite Will and through its Mind, *has to* bear fruit in a perfect Gift: The Gift must contain all the perfections of the Source and its Image whose Love it is (other than being the Source or its Image): It too is an infinite Person ("Holy Spirit") that possesses the same nature and power as the Source and Image from/through which it proceeds. This is the Holy Spirit.

Three in One

Thus, there are Three infinite "Persons" in the Godhead: God as knower and lover, God known, God loved. Consequently, the infinite Mind and Will do not exist as abstractions: they are the Mind and Will OF "someone": in fact of Three: the Infinite Knower and Lover, Its infinite Thought/Image, Its infinite Love/Gift: Father, Son (Word) and Holy Spirit.

Infinite Love

The Three exist in an act of infinite love within the one Godhead: The generation of the infinite "Image" is akin to a Father begetting a Son, without beginning or end, out of infinite-eternal love. Likewise, the Son infinitely and eternally loves the Father who gives everything that he is (other than being Father) to the Son. The Spirit proceeds from and through and AS this common love of Father and Son and in turn loves Father and Son infinitely and eternally.

One

When you ask this question of any spiritual being: are you one being? the question really is: is there one mind and will here? When you ask this of God, the answer is yes, there is only one infinite Mind and Will and therefore only one God. The Three must not be thought of as independent centers of thought or action as in human beings. There are not three states of consciousness or will. They know by the same intellective act and love by the same act of will.

All Three Persons possess the same infinite Mind and Will and all perfections proper to the Godhead: The Father possesses it as sourceless Source, the Son as infinite Image and the Holy Spirit as infinite Gift: but all possess the same divine being.

Postscript

The Holy Trinity is not a matter of puzzling out mathematical or philosophical paradoxes about one and three. It is all about relationship. At the heart of reality lies Heart, a Relationship. In fact, relationship is the greatest mystery in our experience on earth. How did it arise? How did Reality produce relationships? All of our fulfillment in our experience comes from relationship but beyond that there is the question of how relationship as a reality came to be. Once we know that the Source of all that exists is a Relationship, a Relationship of utter and infinite Love, a Heart, everything makes sense. This is what we mean by the Trinity, this is why all the ancient religions grasped its truth, this is why everything in our experience points to it and, finally, this is why God revealed this truth to us in its fullness in the Incarnation.

Now that we have explored three central elements of God 2.0 we can return to the Missing Person who is at the center of it all, the Father.

Time for a Change
Discovering God 2.0

This is the point we have reached thus far:

- We are all creatures of God made in his image who are his children in this respect.
- Jesus invited us to become children of God in a new and unprecedented mode by partaking of the divine nature (2 *Peter* 1:4).
- We can become children in this unimaginably exciting sense only because Jesus has removed the barrier between us and God through his redemptive death and because the Spirit of God enters us – and, of course, this can happen only when we say Yes to Jesus' invitation through our baptism.
- This means that we literally become sons and daughters of the Father because we become adopted brothers and sisters of his Son who are filled with his Holy Spirit and can, therefore, call him *Abba* Father.
- As we see in the Gospels, Jesus could say *Abba* Father because he was of the same divine nature as the Father. As we see in the epistles, we can only say *Abba* Father once we invite the Spirit of God to live in us and thereby become brothers and sisters of Jesus and therefore children of his Father who live with the divine Spirit.

This is the message of God 2.0.

But there is much more we need to know about the Father revealed to us by Jesus in order to truly discover God 2.0. In other words, the revelation of God 2.0 has to be followed by our discovery of this revelation and its incorporation into our lives.

The Bible itself tells us that God reveals himself, his plans and purposes only after human hearts and minds have been suitably prepared and primed: "But when the fullness of time had come, God sent his Son, born of a woman, born under the law, to ransom those under the law, so that we might receive adoption."

(*Galatians* 4:4-5). This is true both of the primordial revelation chronicled in the books of the Bible and of our progressive understanding and assimilation of this revelation.

We talk of discoveries in the world of divine revelation because, as with the great discoveries of science, there are discoveries too in understanding what has been revealed – the discoveries of our lived faith.

The discoveries of the eternal Son and the Holy Spirit and of the Trinity were formalized by the Councils of the first thousand years of Christianity. Subsequently, these became part of the prayer life, public celebration and world vision of the followers of Jesus.

But, as we have noted, the foundational revelation of the Father has yet to be discovered in its fullness. It is this discovery that is our immediate concern.

Our path of discovery requires us to drill deeper into those facets of the Father revealed by Jesus that we have already spoken about: he is prodigal in his love, he is the immeasurably personal *Abba*, he is *our* Father who promises to take care of us at every level.

We review each of these facets in turn – prodigal Father, *Abba* Father, Our Father.

PRODIGAL FATHER

"The man and his wife hid themselves from the LORD God among the trees of the garden. The LORD God then called to the man and asked him: Where are you?" (Genesis 3:8-9)

"And about three o'clock Jesus cried out in a loud voice, "Eli, Eli, lema sabachthani?" which means, "My God, my God, why have you forsaken me?"" (Matthew 27:46)

The story begins at the dawn of creation with the Father's sorrowful call to his son ("Adam, the son of God," *Luke* 3:38), "Where are you?"

It reaches its denouement with the Son's heart-rending cry to his Father, "My God, why have you forsaken me?"

The Garden of Eden has become the Garden of Gethsemane. The act of abandoning the Father was committed by the first Adam; its consequence had to be borne to the fullest degree by the new Adam. The wickedness and woe wrought by one could only be reversed by the pain and suffering of the other.

The Old Testament is an account of the Father seeking the children who have abandoned him. The Father's unconditional, unrequited love is most movingly captured by the prophet Hosea:

> "When Israel was a child I loved him, out of Egypt I called my son. The more I called them, the farther they went from me, sacrificing to the Baals and burning incense to idols. Yet it was I who taught Ephraim to walk, who took them in my arms; but they did not know that I cared for them. I drew them with human cords, with bands of love; I fostered them like those who raise an infant to their cheeks; I bent down to feed them. ...How could I give you up, Ephraim, or deliver you up, Israel? ... My **heart** is overwhelmed, my pity is stirred. I will not give vent to my blazing anger, I will not destroy Ephraim again; For I am God and not a man, the Holy One present among you; I will not come in wrath." (*Hosea* 11: 1-4, 8-9)

The New Testament is a narrative of the Son leading his brothers and sisters back to the Father by sacrificing himself for their sake:

> "The Son of Man did not come to be served but to serve and to give his life as a ransom for many." (*Matthew* 20:28)

> "But when the fullness of time had come, God sent his Son, born of a woman, born under the law, to ransom those under the law, so that we might receive adoption." (*Galatians* 4:4-5)

The Bible itself is a tale of the prodigal love of the Father:

> "For God so loved the world that he gave his only Son, so that everyone who believes in him might not perish but might have eternal life." (*John* 3:16)

Leaving

The Old Testament tells us that God is the father of all humankind: "Have we not all one father? Has not one God created us?" (*Malachi* 2:6). This is why the epistle to the Ephesians declares that there is "one God and Father of all, who is over all and through all and in all." (*Ephesians* 4:6.)

But something went wrong at the start. Something that affected all of us who came after. And its roots lie in our freedom and our unity as a race, as one human family.

This is the tale told by humankind in its myths, ancient narratives and primordial practices.

We read in Greek mythology: "That thou art guiltless of this murder – who should vouch? Nay, nay! Yet indeed a Vengeance from ancient days may have been thine accomplice."

Or take the Book of Genesis:

> "From that tree you shall not eat." "But the serpent said to the woman: 'You certainly will not die! No, God knows well that the moment you eat of it your eyes will be opened and you will be like gods who know what is good and what is bad.'" "The woman answered, "The serpent tricked me into it, so I ate it." (*Genesis* 3: 1-13) "The LORD God therefore banished him from the garden of Eden, to till the ground from which he had been taken." (*Genesis* 3: 14-19, 22-3)

This narrative is not an event in the history of science but the story of the human soul. Its truth is to be found in our own psyches and experience and history as a whole. We are desperately evil. Sin bedevils us all. The deadly sins in all their insane fury weigh each of us down at virtually every instant. Who can deny that guilt and shame play an inordinate role in human life? Or the pattern: first you deliberate, then you perpetrate.

We have already reviewed the hard evidence for all this:

- The most ancient human societies believed that the origin of evil lay in some primordial catastrophe engineered by humanity.
- All pre-Christian religions shared the belief that the original breach created an unbridgeable gulf between us and God.
- The all-pervasive prevalence of the strange practice of sacrifice in every ancient society turned this belief in a divine-human breach into a concrete act.

Sacrifice is the super-theme of human history. Both in primitive and organized societies, sacrifice was *de rigueur*. Its rationale was elaborate. Its performance was linked to expiation (atonement) and reparation. To expiate and to seek reparation means to say "I'm sorry." But "sorry" for what?

Sorry for upsetting the divine order of the universe: this is what they said in ancient India, Persia, China, Israel, et al.

We are told that at the very dawn of its history, the human race said "No" to God: we don't know when, where, how. We just know "that."

This insight is formalized in the doctrine of Original Sin which says simply that evil had its beginning in the abuse of human freedom: and that evil once unleashed leaves its mark in every human psyche.

While sacrifice was the human response to Original Sin, the movement was not just from humankind.

The Hebrew Bible, the Old Testament, shows a divine Father working through the people of Israel to bring all his errant children back to him. This begins with his covenant with Abraham, the father of the Israelite nation: "I swear by myself, declares the LORD ... in your descendants all the nations of the earth shall find blessing – all this because you obeyed my command." (22:16,18)

God is the Father of the family of nations of which Israel is the "first-born."

But the first-born of the Father whose "heart is overwhelmed" is rebellious and fickle, intent on its own destruction:

> "You were unmindful of the Rock that begot you, you forgot the God who gave you birth. The LORD saw and was filled with loathing, provoked by his sons and daughters ... For they are a fickle generation, children with no loyalty in them!" (*Deuteronomy* 32:18-20)

> "Hear, O heavens, and listen, O earth for the LORD speaks: Sons have I raised and reared, but they have rebelled against me! (*Isaiah* 1:2)

> "For this is a rebellious people, deceitful children, Children who refuse to listen to the instruction of the LORD." (*Isaiah* 30:9)

> "Return, rebellious children." (*Jeremiah* 3:14)

The Father does not desire to punish them but *implores* them to repent and return:

> "I have set before you life and death, the blessing and the curse. Choose life, then, that you and your descendants may live, by loving the LORD, your God, obeying his voice, and holding fast to him. For that will mean life for you, a long life for you to live on the land which the LORD swore to your ancestors, to Abraham, Isaac, and Jacob, to give to them." (*Deuteronomy* 30:19-20)

> "I take no pleasure in the death of the wicked, but rather that they turn from their ways and live. Turn, turn from your evil ways! Why should you die, house of Israel?" (*Ezekiel* 33:11)

> "He takes pity according to the abundance of his mercy; He does not willingly afflict or bring grief to human beings." (*Lamentations* 3:32-3)

He also tells the Israelites of the coming of a new, universal and everlasting covenant different from the one originally made with their ancestors:

The "days are coming ... when I will make a new covenant with the house of Israel and the house of Judah. *It will not be like the covenant I made with their ancestors* the day I took them by the hand to lead them out of the land of Egypt. They broke my covenant, though I was their master ... But this is the covenant I will make with the house of Israel after those days ... I will place my law within them, and write it upon their hearts; I will be their God, and they shall be my people." (*Jeremiah* 31:31-3)

"With them I will make an everlasting covenant, never to cease doing good to them; I will put fear of me in their hearts so that they never turn away from me." (*Jeremiah* 32:40)

"They will enter it and remove all its atrocities and abominations. And I will give them another heart and a new spirit I will put within them. From their bodies I will remove the hearts of stone, and give them hearts of flesh, so that they walk according to my statutes, taking care to keep my ordinances. Thus they will be my people, and I will be their God." (*Ezekiel* 11:18-20)

But this new covenant can be instituted only if the original breach is repaired. Isaiah 53 gives us a hint of how this will happen and through whom:

"He had no majestic bearing to catch our eye, no beauty to draw us to him. He was spurned and avoided by men, a man of suffering, knowing pain, like one from whom you turn your face, spurned, and we held him in no esteem. Yet it was our pain that he bore, our sufferings he endured. We thought of him as stricken, struck down by God and afflicted, but he was pierced for our sins, crushed for our iniquity. He bore the punishment that makes us whole, by his wounds we were healed. We had all gone astray like sheep, all following our own way; But the LORD laid upon him the guilt of us all. Though harshly treated, he submitted and did not open his mouth; Like a lamb led to slaughter or a sheep silent before shearers, he did not open his mouth. Seized and condemned, he was taken away. Who would have thought any more of his destiny? For he was cut off from the land of the living, struck for the sins of his people. He was given a grave among the wicked, a burial place with evildoers, though he had done no wrong, nor was deceit found in his mouth. But it was the LORD's will to crush him with pain. By making his life as a reparation offering he shall see his offspring, shall lengthen his days, and the LORD's will shall be accomplished through him. Because of his anguish he shall see the light; because of his knowledge he shall be content; My servant, the just one, shall justify the many, their iniquity he shall bear. My servant, the just one, shall justify the many, their iniquity he shall bear. Therefore I will give him his portion among the many, and he shall divide the spoils with the mighty, Because he surrendered himself to death, was counted among the transgressors, Bore the sins of many, and interceded for the transgressors." (*Isaiah* 53:2-12)

Returning

Which takes us to the New Testament, i.e., "the New Covenant."

The very name of Jesus tells us that his mission is to take us back to the Father: "You are to name him Jesus, because he will save his people from their sins" (*Matthew* 1:21).

From the very beginning there was no doubt as to the meaning of this mission. "Just as through one transgression condemnation came upon all, so through one righteous act acquittal and life came to all" (*Romans* 5:18). The suffering for the sins of humanity that Jesus took on himself was for sins past, present, and future – "Through his suffering, my servant shall justify many, and their guilt he shall bear. ... He shall take away the sins of many, and win pardon for their offenses" (*Isaiah* 53:11–12). When Jesus asks Saul, "why are you persecuting me?" we are given to understand that this persecution of Christians personally afflicts him. In fact, those who reject the faith they had once accepted, apostate Christians, "are re-crucifying the Son of God for themselves." (*Hebrews* 6:6).

Only Jesus' identity as the divine Son incarnate makes sense of his being able to cure the breach.

The solution to the problem of Original Sin is a redemptive act that can be performed only by someone who is both divine and human.

We have seen why this is the case.

The slightest offence against God who is infinite goodness and holiness is infinite in its impact: God's infinite Goodness cannot, by its very nature, co-exist with the slightest evil and so the slightest rejection of God means total separation.

Thus humanity's "Fall" created an unbridgeable gulf between Creator and creatures. Only an atoning sacrifice of infinite value could re-open the path to God. And it would have to be a sacrifice performed by the offending party: Adam: humanity. And yet only an infinite Person could perform a sacrifice of infinite value.

There was no solution to this problem from the standpoint of divine law and logic. But then there is also the reality of the Father's love.

And the Father's solution was as ingenious as it was poignant: An infinite Person would take on a human nature and atone for humanity's Original Sin. As damnation came from disobedience, salvation would come from perfect obedience. And obedience in a world of sin and evil meant suffering and death. As we saw, "God so loved the world that he gave his only Son, so that everyone who believes in him might not perish but might have eternal life." (*John* 3:16).

To understand the possibility of one man taking on the consequences of the actions of other humans, we have only to reflect on the "solidarity" of all humanity in the consequences of sin. The choices of a father shape and affect his children just as the acts of a head of state affect and involve the nation as a whole. But the same cause-and-effect web that connects negative choices and their consequences also links positive choices with their consequences. And that is why it was possible for Jesus—the new Adam—to be the redeemer of humanity.

The liberation from sin offered by Jesus is unprecedented. Stanley Jaki notes that the writers of the Old Testament "agonized over their sins, over their offenses to God's holiness," but they do not show the same "certainty about having gained forgiveness" as Paul, Peter and John in their epistles. These epistles "go far beyond what is found in Psalm 50 (51), the Miserere, and in Psalm 129 (130), the *De profundis*. In both there is hope but no certainty that one's sins have been forgiven." The forgiveness and purification Jesus offers is illustrated in the assurance given to Peter "by Jesus that he and the other apostles were all clean after He had washed their feet. There was enough pagan lore in Judaea for the apostles to perceive that in Jesus the divine appeared in a sense infinitely superior to the best which the pagan gods evoked. ... The Incarnate God in whom the Church wanted to keep faith was wholly different from those gods because Jesus himself noted, and most emphatically, that no one could accuse him of any sin."[1]

There are three universal desires:

- to be absolved of guilt and shame;
- to love and be loved;
- to make sense of and cope with suffering.

Jesus absolved, he loved, and his suffering gave meaning to all suffering.

Backstory

The Father's unconditional love for us, his Paternal Heart, underlies the whole Incarnation of the Son of God:

> "God is love. In this way the love of God was revealed to us: God sent his only Son into the world so that we might have life through him. In this is love: not that we have loved God, but that he loved us and sent his Son as expiation for our sins." (1 *John* 4:8-10)

His love impels him to make us children of God:

> "See what love the Father has bestowed on us that we may be called the children of God." (1 *John* 3:1)

In his mercy, he rescues us from the consequences of our evil

> "But God, who is rich in mercy, because of the great love he had for us, even when we were dead in our transgressions, brought us to life with Christ." (*Ephesians* 2:4-5)

He bestows on us the imperishable inheritance of Heaven:

> "Blessed be the God and Father of our Lord Jesus Christ, who in his great mercy gave us a new birth to a living hope through the resurrection of Jesus Christ from the dead, to an inheritance that is imperishable, undefiled, and unfading, kept in heaven for you." (1*Peter* 1:3-4)

He rushes to lovingly receive those who reject him and yet repent and return:

> "He got up and went back to his father. While he was still a long way off, his father caught sight of him, and was filled with compassion. He ran to his son, embraced him and kissed him. His son said to him, 'Father, I have sinned against heaven and against you; I no longer deserve to be called your son.' But his father ordered his servants, 'Quickly bring the finest robe and put it on him; put a ring on his finger and sandals on his feet. Take the fattened calf and slaughter it. Then let us celebrate with a feast, because this son of mine was dead, and has come to life again; he was lost, and has been found.' Then the celebration began." (*Luke* 15:10-24)

All that we receive comes from him:

> "Every perfect gift is from above, coming down from the Father of lights." (*James* 1:17)

He loves us to the point of watching over every infinitesimal detail of our being:

> "Are not five sparrows sold for two small coins? Yet not one of them has escaped the notice of God. Even the hairs of your head have all been counted. Do not be afraid. You are worth more than many sparrows." (*Luke* 12:6-7)

> "Look at the birds in the sky; they do not sow or reap, they gather nothing into barns, yet your heavenly Father feeds them. Are not you more important than they?" (*Matthew* 6:26)

He refuses his beloved children nothing:

> "If you then, who are wicked, know how to give good gifts to your children, how much more will your heavenly Father give good things to those who ask him." (*Matthew* 7:11)

> "So do not worry and say, 'What are we to eat?' or 'What are we to drink?' or 'What are we to wear?' All these things the pagans seek. Your heavenly Father knows that you need them all. But seek first the kingdom [of God] and his righteousness, and all these things will be given you besides." (*Matthew* 6:31-33)

ABBA FATHER

"Jesus answered and said to him, "Amen, amen, I say to you, no one can see the kingdom of God without being born from above." (John 3:3)

"As proof that you are children, God sent the Spirit of his Son into our hearts, crying out, 'Abba, Father!'" (Galatians 4:6).

"I live, no longer I, but Christ lives in me." (Galatians 2:20).

"We are the offspring of God." (Acts 17:39).

Children of the Father

In recognizing God 2.0, we become aware of the invitation to become Homo sapiens 2.0.

God is the Father of all humanity as Creator.

He is also the Father of a specific people, the House of Israel which was tasked with preserving and propagating the truths revealed to them. "LORD, you are our father; ... do not remember our crimes forever; look upon us, who are all your people!" (*Isaiah* 64:7-8)

But with the incarnation of his eternal Son, he invites all of us to live with the divine Life, to "share in the divine nature" (2 *Peter* 1:4), to receive "the Spirit of his Son into our hearts, crying out, 'Abba, Father!'"

What happens is nothing less than the re-invention of the human person and human destiny. Those who are baptized into Christ are "re-invented" as "the offspring of God."

Fount of Rebirth

Jesus taught that baptism is the entry point into the divine Life:

> "No one can enter the kingdom of God without being born of water and Spirit." (John 3:5)

> "Whoever believes and is baptized will be saved; whoever does not believe will be condemned." (Mark 16:16).

Through baptism we are "clothed" with Christ and become children of his Father:

> "For through faith you are all children of God in Christ Jesus. For all of you who were baptized into Christ have clothed yourselves with Christ. (*Galatians* 3:26-7).

We are re-purposed and reprogrammed at this fountain of rebirth. "Repent and be baptized, every one of you, in the name of Jesus Christ for the forgiveness of your sins; and you will receive the gift of the holy Spirit." (*Acts* 2:38) We are given new powers (*Joel* 3:1, *Acts* 2:17). These "powers" include the virtues of faith, hope and charity and the gifts and fruits of the Holy Spirit.

In the new divine order, human destiny is oriented to salvation – eternal union with the Father through Jesus the Way, the Truth and the Life to whom we are led by the Spirit.

Liberation from the consequences of sin

Jesus liberates us not just from sin but its consequences. Under the Old Covenant, "punishment for their parents' wickedness" was passed on to their "children and children's children to the third and fourth generation!" (*Exodus* 34:7) But under the New Covenant, the Lord says, "I will forgive their evildoing and remember their sins no more." (*Hebrews* 8:12)

A Free Gift

The grace we receive from the Father for faith and salvation is entirely a gift that we do not and cannot merit. We are not saved by works whether these be the ceremonial or judicial decrees of the Mosaic Law or our responses to the fundamental moral law laid out in the Ten Commandments. We are saved by grace: the Power of God, the Holy Spirit, acting in us. But this grace is not forced on us: we must accede to it, welcome it, let it "in."

Accepting the Invitation

This emphasis on the link between our choices here and our destiny hereafter is highlighted in the entire New Testament. Salvation is a state of deliverance from evil and transformation of our being. It commences in the here and now and reaches its full glory in the direct presence of the Father. Eternal life and the Kingdom of the Father are of this world and the next. Everything is interconnected.

Believed from the Beginning

This salvation vision is not something derived from cobbling together disparate biblical verses. Rather, it is the teaching consistently held by those who followed Jesus from the very beginning: it is not recent and it is not novel. It is primal and organic. It is rooted in the Word of God as interpreted and proclaimed even before the canon of the New Testament was fixed.

The Obedience of Faith

Once we accept and live in the grace of God, we are required also to obey his Ten Commandments and the moral law he established. The Apostle Paul calls us to "the obedience of faith." (*Romans* 1:5, 16:26). This obedience is a call to holiness: "Let us cleanse ourselves from every defilement of flesh and spirit, making holiness perfect in the fear of God." (2 *Corinthians* 7:1) The "obedience of faith" is divinely powered: "So then, my beloved, obedient as you have always been, ... work out your salvation with fear and trembling. For God is the one who, for his good purpose, works in you both to desire and to work." (*Philippians* 2:12)

Saying No

Of course, Jesus warned us that "Not everyone who says to me, 'Lord, Lord,' will enter the kingdom of heaven, but only the one who does the will of my Father in heaven." (*Matthew* 7:21). He also said, "For the Son of Man is going to come in the glory of his Father with his angels, and, when he does, he will reward each one according to his behavior." (*Matthew* 16:27).

Paul gives the same warning: "Your stubborn refusal to repent is only adding to the anger God will have toward you on that day of anger when his just judgments will be made known. He will repay each one as his works deserve. For those who sought renown and honor and immortality by always doing good there will be eternal life; for the unsubmissive who refused to take truth for their guide and took depravity instead, there will be anger and fury." (*Romans* 2:5-8)

The second epistle of Peter makes it clear that Christians can be "lost" if they fall away: "There will be false teachers among you, who will introduce destructive heresies and even deny the Master who *ransomed them*, bringing swift destruction on themselves." (2 *Peter* 2:1)

OUR FATHER

*"Our Father **knows what you need before you ask him**. This is how you are to pray: Our Father in heaven, hallowed be your name, your kingdom come, your will be done, on earth as in heaven. Give us today our daily bread; and forgive us our debts, as we forgive our debtors; and do not subject us to the final test, but deliver us from the evil one." (Matthew 6:8-13)*

Jesus' revelation that God is *Abba*, a father at the most intimate level, is accompanied by his proclamation that we are to address him as *our* Father. A father who protects and provides for us.

This proclamation is most famously embodied in the "Our Father" prayer.

The "Our Father" is the most important prayer of all because it is the Lord's prayer, the prayer that God incarnate has asked of us. *"Unlike all the prayers of the past which were formal prayers of the community addressed to God under one of his titles – but never by name except on the Day of Atonement – this is a personal prayer where the individual addresses the Father by name."* It is one-on-one. It is from a child to its Father.

The most immediate practical application of the prayer is the command to entrust all our desires and needs to *our* Father. We are never to worry about anything. Jesus specifies this right at the start of the Our Father prayer: *"Our Father knows what you need before you ask him."*

The Lord's Prayer in the Gospel of Luke is followed by the "ask and you will receive" commands culminating in this most memorable promise: "How much more will the Father in heaven give the holy Spirit to those who ask him?" (*Luke* 11:13)

The Our Father's state of surrender and total trust is detailed in Psalms 91 and 23 and consummated in the teaching of Jesus.

Our Father invites us into the safety of his Heart – GodSpace – while leading us through the Valley of the Shadow. Every care, every worry, all our needs and aspirations must be handed to him. He refuses us nothing if we truly surrender to him.

"There is Nothing I Shall Lack"

Divine Plan

"For I know well the plans I have in mind for you ... plans for your welfare and not for woe, so as to give you a future of hope. When you call me, and come and pray to me, I will listen to you." (*Jeremiah* 29:11-12)

Deliverance

"Many are the troubles of the righteous, but the LORD delivers him from them all. He watches over all his bones; not one of them shall be broken." (*Psalm* 34:21)

"God is our refuge and our strength, an ever-present help in distress. Thus we do not fear." (*Psalm* 46:2-3)

"In their distress they cried to the LORD, who saved them in their peril; He brought them forth from darkness and the shadow of death and broke their chains asunder." (*Psalm* 107:13-14)

Fear Nothing/Do Not Worry

"I command you: be firm and steadfast! Do not fear nor be dismayed, for the LORD, your God, is with you wherever you go." (*Joshua* 1:9)

"Do not fear: I am with you; do not be anxious: I am your God. I will strengthen you, I will help you, I will uphold you with my victorious right hand." (*Isaiah* 41:10)

"Do not fear, for I have redeemed you; I have called you by name: you are mine." (*Isaiah* 43:1)

The Battle is not Ours but God's

"For it is the LORD, your God, who goes with you to fight for you against your enemies and give you victory." (*Deuteronomy* 20:4)

"Do not fear or be dismayed ... for the battle is not yours but God's.'" (II *Chronicles* 20:15)

"All this multitude, too, shall learn that it is not by sword or spear that the LORD saves. For the battle belongs to the LORD, who shall deliver [the adversary] into our hands." (1 *Samuel* 17:47)

"The horse is equipped for the day of battle, but victory is the LORD's." (*Proverbs* 21:31)

"What then shall we say to this? If God is for us, who can be against us?" (*Romans* 8:31)

In God I Trust

"My foes turn back when I call on you. This I know: God is on my side. I praise the word of God, I praise the word of the LORD. In God I trust, I do not fear." (*Psalm* 56:10-12)

"Trust in the LORD with all your heart, on your own intelligence do not rely; In all your ways be mindful of him, and he will make straight your paths." (*Proverbs* 3:5-6)

Ask and Receive

"When you call me, and come and pray to me, I will listen to you." (*Jeremiah* 29:12)

"Before they call, I will answer; while they are yet speaking, I will hear." (*Isaiah* 65:24)

"When you began your petition, an answer was given which I have come to announce, because you are beloved." (*Daniel* 9:23)

"Jesus told his disciples a parable about the necessity for them to pray always without becoming weary. He said, 'There was a judge in a certain town who neither feared God nor respected any human being. And a widow in that town used to come to him and say, 'Render a just decision for me against my adversary.' For a long time the judge was unwilling, but eventually he thought, 'While it is true that I neither fear God nor respect any human being, because this widow keeps bothering me I shall deliver a just decision for her lest she finally come and strike me.' The Lord said, 'Pay attention to what the dishonest judge says. Will not God then secure the rights of his chosen ones who call out to him day and night? Will he be slow to answer them? I tell you, he will see to it that justice is done for them speedily.'" (*Luke* 18:1-8)

"Jesus said to his disciples: 'Suppose one of you has a friend to whom he goes at midnight and says, 'Friend, lend me three loaves of bread, for a friend of mine has arrived at my house from a journey and I have nothing to offer him,' and he says in reply from within, 'Do not bother me; the door has already been locked and my children and I are already in bed. I cannot get up to give you anything.' I tell you, if he does not get up to give him the loaves because of their friendship, he will get up to give him whatever he needs because of his persistence.

"'And I tell you, ask and you will receive; seek and you will find; knock and the door will be opened to you. For everyone who asks, receives; and the one who seeks, finds; and to the one who knocks, the door will be opened. What father among you would hand his son a snake when he asks for a fish? Or hand him a scorpion when he asks for an egg? If you then, who are wicked, know how to give good gifts to your children, how much more will the Father in heaven give the Holy Spirit to those who ask him?'" (*Luke* 11:5-13)

"Amen, I say to you, if you have faith the size of a mustard seed, you will say to this mountain, 'Move from here to there,' and it will move. Nothing will be impossible for you." (*Matthew* 17: 20)

"All that you ask for in prayer, believe that you will receive it and it shall be yours." (*Mark* 11: 24)

"If you remain in me and my words remain in you, ask for whatever you want and it will be done for you." (*John* 15:7)

"He who did not spare his own Son but handed him over for us all, how will he not also give us everything else along with him?" (*Romans* 8:32)

"My God will fully supply whatever you need, in accord with his glorious riches in Christ Jesus." (*Philippians* 4:19)

Do Not Doubt

"Immediately Jesus stretched out his hand and caught Peter, and said to him, 'O you of little faith, why did you doubt?' After they got into the boat, the wind died down." (*Matthew* 14: 31-2)

"But he should ask in faith, not doubting, for the one who doubts is like a wave of the sea that is driven and tossed about by the wind. For that person must not suppose that he will receive anything from the Lord, since he is a man of two minds, unstable in all his ways." (*James* 1:6-8)

A Peace of HIS Mind

"Peace I leave with you; my peace I give to you. Not as the world gives do I give it to you." (*John* 14:27)

"The God of peace be with all of you." (*Romans* 15:33)

"The God of peace will quickly crush Satan under your feet." (*Romans* 16:20)

Guard Your Heart

"Cast your care upon the LORD, who will give you support. He will never allow the righteous to stumble." (*Psalm* 55:23)

"Cast all your worries upon him because he cares for you." (1 *Peter* 5:7)

"With all vigilance guard your heart, for in it are the sources of life." (*Proverbs* 4:23)

"Have no anxiety at all, but in everything, by prayer and petition, with thanksgiving, make your requests known to God. Then the peace of God that surpasses all understanding will guard your hearts and minds in Christ Jesus." (*Philippians* 4:6-7).

The Father offers us a "deal": if we do what he asks of us, then he promises to watch our back!

And this is what we have to do. This is all we have to do:
Trust the Father totally to provide us with everything we need and never fear anything or be worried.

Here is the payback:
He will take care of all our needs.

We just entrust all our needs, worries, problems, crises, challenges, obstacles to the Father and it becomes his responsibility to resolve them all.

In the measure we trust, in that measure we receive. And it is not a matter of trusting blindly but trusting with our eyes wide open: trusting in the sense of acting by divine directive at every instant.

This is the simple but extraordinary message running through all the books of the Bible. Is it doable? Does it work? The heroes and heroines of the Bible bear witness to its transcendent power. Millions of the followers of Jesus through the centuries and in the present day testify to its truth.

Every time we pray for something, we must remember that God is omnipotent, all-powerful, almighty. Hence we are told that "nothing will be impossible for God." (*Luke* 1:37) and "for God all things are possible." (*Matthew* 19:26). But we can unlock and unleash his Power on our behalf only if we trust so completely in him that we will not let our fear and worry block the pipeline that transports it.

The twenty third Psalm lays out the Father's Promise:

> "The LORD is my shepherd; there is nothing I lack. In green pastures he makes me lie down; to still waters he leads me; he restores my soul. He guides me along right paths for the sake of his name. Even though I walk through the valley of the shadow of death, I will fear no evil, for you are with me; your rod and your staff comfort me. You set a table before me in front of my enemies; You anoint my head with oil; my cup overflows. Indeed, goodness and mercy will pursue me all the days of my life; I will dwell in the house of the LORD for endless days."

> His protection and provision, his Power and Providence "will pursue me all the days of my life."

Jesus confirms and amplifies the Promise in his Sermon on the Mount:

> "Therefore I tell you, *do not worry* about your life, what you will eat (or drink), or about your body, what you will wear. Is not life more than food and the body more than clothing? Look at the birds in the sky; they

do not sow or reap, they gather nothing into barns, yet your heavenly Father feeds them. Are not you more important than they? Can any of you by worrying add a single moment to your life-span? Why are you anxious about clothes? Learn from the way the wild flowers grow. They do not work or spin. But I tell you that not even Solomon in all his splendor was clothed like one of them. If God so clothes the grass of the field, which grows today and is thrown into the oven tomorrow, will he not much more provide for you, O you of little faith? So *do not worry* and say, 'What are we to eat?' or 'What are we to drink?' or 'What are we to wear?' All these things the pagans seek. Your heavenly Father knows that you need them all. But seek first the kingdom (of God) and his righteousness, and all these things will be given you besides. *Do not worry* about tomorrow; tomorrow will take care of itself. Sufficient for a day is its own evil." (*Matthew* 6:25-34)

Jesus says, "Do not worry" three times – just in case we do not get the message!

But why does the Father need us to trust him before acting?

First, the entire divine plan of creation is built on love and love cannot exist without freedom. God has instituted a framework of freedom and will work through it. He cannot coerce us into loving him because this would not be love: if we see him in all his glory, we cannot but adore him. But that would not be love. To love him, we have to meet him *heart to heart*: we have to respond to his still small voice: we have to give ourselves to him as he gives himself to us. His revelation makes it clear that God cannot help us until we trust in him. Jesus "was not able to perform any mighty deed there... He was amazed at their lack of faith" (*Mark* 6:5-6) "He did not work many mighty deeds there because of their lack of faith" (*Matthew* 13:58)

Secondly, we are made for Heaven. But to enter Heaven, we have to become heavenly. We have to change and be changed – radically. We have to become new persons, our *hearts* transformed. A central element of our transformation is changing our entire way of seeing things: we should rely only on divine Providence and fear nothing. We have to be like little children, said Jesus. We have to trust our Heavenly Father who will give us our daily bread.

There is a third touching answer. The Father has feelings because the Father is *Heart*. A father is hurt when his child does not trust him to provide for her. Likewise, our heavenly Father is hurt when we entertain the slightest doubt about his ability to take care of us. An accurate measure of our love for God is the degree of our trust in his Providence. To the extent to which we cast our cares on him asking him to resolve them, to that extent we truly believe he loves us. Not to trust him is to doubt his love. It also means that our love for him is limited since we will not take him at his Word. The Father wants to take us to Heaven. But he can only do this if we trust him to provide for us on the way and protect us from all obstacles.

The Promised Land

"This is my beloved Son, with whom I am well pleased." (Matthew 3:17)

"'This is my Son, my beloved, with whom I am well pleased.' We ourselves heard this voice come from heaven while we were with him on the holy mountain." (2 Peter 1:17-18)

*"Abba, Father, **all things are possible to you**." (Mark 14:36)*

*"For those who are led by the Spirit of God are children of God. For you did not receive a spirit of slavery **to fall back into fear**, but you received a spirit of adoption, through which we cry, "Abba, Father!" (Romans 8:14-15)*

*"God is love, and whoever remains in love remains in God and God in him. ... There is no fear in love, but **perfect love drives out fear**." (1 John 4:16,18)*

*As **proof that you are children**, God sent the spirit of his Son into our hearts, crying out, 'Abba, Father!' So you are no longer a slave but a child, and if a child **then also an heir**, through God." (Galatians 4:6-7).*

We are heirs. Our inheritance is the Promised Land. The Promised Land is the Kingdom of our Father. We have only to take possession of our inheritance. The sole obstacle is our own falling "back into fear." But the Holy Spirit overcomes fear by "proving" that we are indeed "children" and therefore heirs as our hearts cry out 'Abba, Father!' And the Father's "perfect love" for us continually "drives out fear."

Through it all, we simply have to trust totally and be patient. "After patient waiting, Abraham obtained the promise." (*Hebrews* 6:15) We in turn are called to be "imitators of those who, through *faith and patience*, are *inheriting the promises*." (*Hebrews* 6:12)

In our journey of faith, we must move from simply seeing God as our Almighty Creator and Protector to recognizing him as our beloved Father. The Yahweh who draws his people to the physical Promised Land is now seen to be our immeasurably intimate *Abba*. He rushes out to us his wayward children and draws us into his Paternal Heart through the Spirit of his Son. "God sent the spirit of his Son into our hearts, crying out, 'Abba, Father!'"

Entering the Promised Land means unconditionally accepting the Promises of God and thereby sharing in the Power of God. "He has bestowed on us the precious and very great promises, so that through them you may come to share in the divine nature." (2 *Peter* 1:4).

These are "the precious and very great promises:"

> forgiveness,
> redemption,
> mercy,
> eternal ecstasy,
> glory,
> protection,
> provision,
> peace that surpasses all understanding,
> love beyond all telling,
> life in all its fullness,
> joy than no one can take from us.

We have only to surrender to our Father. We have only to trust in Jesus. We have only to be filled with the Holy Spirit.

This revelation of our dearest *Abba* transforms the entire prior understanding of religion and God. It was what we might call a "paradigm-shift." Accordingly, beginning with the "Our Father" taught by Jesus, the first Christians addressed and experienced God as "*Abba*." For the first time it was possible to have a relationship with God. It was indeed a personal relationship with Our Father. And it is our relationship status that determines our eternal destiny. "Unless you turn and become like children, you will not enter the kingdom of heaven." (*Matthew* 18:3)

Further, only in seeing God as our loving Father and experiencing his love can we trust totally without fear of any kind. "There is no fear in love." Our whole life has to be centered on becoming aware of the infinite love of our Father and surrendering our needs, our worries, our hopes to him. Once we live and move and have our being in the infinite love of our *Abba*, "there is nothing I shall fear."

There is nothing more to fear, nothing to worry about, nothing that is out of reach. I am in my Father's House. I am a temple of the Holy Spirit. I live no longer "I" for "Christ lives in me." (Galatians 2:20). And, "whoever is joined to the Lord becomes one spirit with him." (I Corinthians 6:17). I am "no longer a slave but a child" of God and because I am his child I am also "an heir." (Galatians 4: 7).

A Time for Action
Homo Sapiens 2.0

Retaining our vision of the Father is a continuing challenge. But there is no point in recognizing the reality of the Father if we do not live in communion with him. Those who call him *Abba* are those who accept the redemption gifted by the Son and the indwelling of the Spirit. They live with the life of God. They become Homo sapiens 2.0. What difference does this make and should make to our everyday life?

From Knowing to Doing

"Out of the ground the LORD God made grow every tree that was delightful to look at and good for food, with the tree of life in the middle of the garden." (Genesis 2:9)

"Then the angel showed me the river of life-giving water … On either side of the river grew the tree of life." (Revelation 22:1-2)

"The mystery hidden from ages and from generations past. But now it has been manifested to his holy ones." (Colossians 1:36)

"So, too, it is written, 'The first man, Adam, became a living being,' the last Adam a life-giving spirit.'" (1 Corinthians 15:45)

"Through him was life, and this life was the light of the human race." (John 1:3-4)

"For just as the Father has life in himself, so also he gave to his Son the possession of life in himself." (John 5:26)

"And this is the testimony: God gave us eternal life, and this life is in his Son. Whoever possesses the Son has life; whoever does not possess the Son of God does not have life. I write these things to you so that you may know that you have eternal life, you who believe in the name of the Son of God." (1 John 5:11-13)

Irenaeus of Lyons: "The Word of God, Jesus Christ, on account of his great love for mankind, became what we are in order to make us what he is himself."[9]

Cyril of Alexandria: "We have all become partakers of Him, and have Him in ourselves through the Spirit. For this reason we have become partakers of the divine nature."[10]

Augustine: "But this is by grace of adoption and not of the nature of our begetter."[11]

God 2.0 is accompanied by the similarly revolutionary revelation of Homo sapiens 2.0.

The Father's Plan is nothing less than to adopt us! As his creations, we are already his children in our human nature. Further, through his covenant with Abraham, Israel as a nation became his child in his blueprint of salvation.

But both kinds of paternity were at the level of human life.

Jesus revealed that we were to become children of the Father living with his kind of Life.

Sharing in the Divine Nature

The Father's ultimate goal was for us to "share in the divine nature" (2 *Peter* 1:4). It was to birth a new race living with the Life of God, the Holy Spirit. This was made possible by our becoming brothers and sisters of the divine Son of the Father in his human nature.

> "Blessed be the God and Father of our Lord Jesus Christ, who has blessed us in Christ with every spiritual blessing in the heavens, as he chose us in him, before the foundation of the world ...In love he destined us for adoption to himself through Jesus Christ." (*Ephesians* 1:3-5)

> "See what love the Father has bestowed on us that we may be called the children of God. Yet so we are. ... Beloved, we are God's children now." (1 *John* 3:1-2).

Revealing the Divine Plan

In speaking of the divine plan, Jesus revealed that:

- Human destiny is divinely oriented – our ultimate destiny is either eternal union with God or eternal separation from him and it is we who choose between the two options
- Salvation is freely offered – Jesus gave his life as "a ransom for many" so that we might have the opportunity to choose eternal union with God
- The Life of God is given to all who surrender themselves to Its Source – through his life, death and resurrection, Jesus invites us to live with his Life:

> "To those who did accept him he gave power to become children of God, to those who believe in his name, who were born not by natural generation nor by human choice nor by a man's decision but of God." (*John* 1:12-13)

> "Whoever is joined to the Lord becomes one spirit with him." (I *Corinthians* 6:17).

The Father sends the Son for our redemption from sin. The Father sends the Spirit through the Son for our sanctification and salvation.

As we have seen, it is when we live with the Life of God that we can call God "Abba":

> "God sent the Spirit of his Son into our hearts, crying out, 'Abba, Father!'" (*Galatians* 4:6).

To life with the Life of God is to live in his universe.

GODSPACE
(The Kingdom of the Father on earth)

Strewn through the Old Testament are hints of a new world of space and time transcending and yet touching down in our here-and-now. In the New Testament we learn that this is the Kingdom of the Father on earth – GodSpace.

Once we recognize God as our Father and accept his invitation to become his children, the next step is to enter GodSpace.

GodSpace is

- ❖ a place – a shelter provided by the Father;
- ❖ a time – an abiding in the Father; and
- ❖ a recurring activity – a perpetual heart-to-Heart encounter with the Father.

GodSpace is our plunge into the Heart of the Father. We close our eyes. We place our hearts and minds, our thoughts and feelings, before our Father, our

Savior, our Comforter. We enter the Abode of the Most High. We trust and we surrender, we ask and we receive and, finally, we feel and we touch the Love that IS.

Thee three dimensions of this new God-world, are its space, its time and its activity of encounter and communion. Its space is the Secret Place of the Most High. Its time transcends the terrestrial and the temporal: it is not a question of past, present or future but a state of being present with and in the Father. And its activity is centered on talking and listening to the Father as often as practicable.

GodSpace is possible only for those who surrender to the Father, trust him in all things and speak to him from the depth of their being.

The Secret Place

The new "world" with its own space and time is highlighted in Psalm 91. The Psalm lays out the architecture, foundations and superstructure of "the secret place:"

> "You who dwell in *the shelter of the Most High*, who abide in *the shade of the Almighty*, Say to the LORD, 'My refuge and fortress, my God in whom I trust.' He will rescue you from the fowler's snare, from the destroying plague, He will *shelter you with his pinions*, and *under his wings you may take refuge*; his faithfulness is a protecting shield. You shall not fear the terror of the night nor the arrow that flies by day, Nor the pestilence that roams in darkness, nor the plague that ravages at noon. Though a thousand fall at your side, ten thousand at your right hand, near you it shall not come. You need simply watch; the punishment of the wicked you will see. Because you have *the LORD* for your refuge and have made *the Most High your stronghold*, No evil shall befall you, no affliction come near *your tent*. For he commands his angels with regard to you, to guard you wherever you go. With their hands they shall support you, lest you strike your foot against a stone. You can tread upon the asp and the viper, trample the lion and the dragon. Because *he clings to me* I will deliver him; because he knows my name *I will set him on high*. He will call upon me and I will answer; I will be with him in distress; I will deliver him and give him honor. With length of days I will satisfy him, *and fill him with my saving power*."

The "shelter of the Most High" means "hiding place" says the footnote to the Psalm in the New American Bible. The *Brown-Driver-Briggs Hebrew Lexicon* defines it as "hiding place, shelter, *secret place*." A "shelter" is a place of safety.

The "secret place" of the Father should change our perspectives and priorities, our thoughts and actions. In this space, we find protection from crises, disasters, enemies, afflictions; we find long life and provision, peace and joy; and we will be filled with [his] "saving power." We are asked to "dwell" in this space: to make it our home.

We are told about the "secret place" of the Father's shelter in other parts of the Old Testament:

> "For God will hide me in his shelter in time of trouble, He will conceal me in the cover of his tent; and set me high upon a rock." (*Psalm* 27:5)

> "You hide them in the shelter of your presence, safe from scheming enemies. You conceal them in your tent, away from the strife of tongues." (*Psalm* 31:21)

> "Therefore every loyal person should pray to you in time of distress. Though flood waters threaten, they will never reach him. You are my shelter; you guard me from distress; with joyful shouts of deliverance you surround me." (*Psalm* 32:6-7)

> "For you are my refuge, a tower of strength against the foe. Let me dwell in your tent forever, take refuge in the shelter of your wings." (*Psalm* 61:4-5)

We hear echoes of the "shade of the Almighty" in the divine encounter with Moses: "Here, continued the LORD, is a place near me where you shall station yourself on the rock. When my glory passes I will set you in the cleft of the rock and will cover you with my hand until I have passed by." (*Exodus* 33:21-2)

The prophet Isaiah writes, "Go, my people, enter your chambers, and close the doors behind you; Hide yourselves for a brief moment, until the wrath is past." (*Isaiah* 26:20)

In the Secret Place, the Father speaks to us in a "still, small voice:"

> Then the LORD said: Go out and stand on the mountain before the LORD; the LORD will pass by. There was a strong and violent wind rending the mountains and crushing rocks before the LORD—but the LORD was not in the wind; after the wind, an earthquake—but the LORD was not in the earthquake; after the earthquake, fire—but the LORD was not in the fire; after the fire, a light silent sound. When he heard this, Elijah hid his face in his cloak and went out and stood at the entrance of the cave. A voice said to him, Why are you here, Elijah? (I *Kings* 19:11-13)

The climax comes with Jesus' revelation that the Secret Place is where we dwell *in him and his Father and his Spirit* and the Triune God dwells *in us*:

> "Remain *in me, as I remain in you.* ... If you remain in me and my words remain in you, ask for whatever you want and it will be done for you." (*John* 15:4,7)
>
> "Jesus answered and said to him, "Whoever loves me will keep my word, and my Father will love him, and *we will come to him and make our dwelling with him.*" (*John* 14:23)
>
> "Do you not know that *you are the temple of God*, and that *the Spirit of God dwells in you*? If anyone destroys God's temple, God will destroy that person; for the temple of God, which you are, is holy." (1 *Corinthians* 3:16-7)

The promises of *Psalm* 91 are now applied to the followers of Jesus who, through him and the Holy Spirit, become the children of the Father:

> "Behold, I have given you the power 'to tread upon serpents' and scorpions and upon the full force of the enemy and nothing will harm you. Nevertheless, do not rejoice because the spirits are subject to you, but rejoice because *your names are written in heaven.*" (*Luke* 10: 19.20)
>
> "Are they not all ministering spirits sent to serve, for the sake of *those who are to inherit salvation?*" (*Hebrews* 1:14)
>
> "But when you pray, go to your inner room, close the door, and pray to your Father in secret. And *your Father who sees in secret* will repay you." (*Matthew* 6:6)

The most profound and potent meditation on "the secret place" comes from Gregory of Nyssa "who all have called the father of fathers" (Second Council of Nicea). Gregory identifies the cleft/hole in the rock where Moses encounters God with "the secret place" of *Psalm* 91 and the rock itself with Jesus. Those who remain faithful to Jesus live in this "heavenly house not made with hands."

The upshot of the biblical revelation is simply this: we are invited to be with and in the Father in a divine space in which we are preserved from all harm and filled with divine Power.

So how can we do this and how do we know we are "there?"

We must tune ourselves into the Love that IS. We must begin to feel the Love of the Father at every instant in every experience. We must connect at the level of the heart.

We close our eyes and look back at our lives: an hour ago, a day ago, across the years. We see his Love reaching out to us through a thousand people, the food and drink and habitation we have received, our health, our family, our friends.

As we focus on each breath we take, we realize that it is his Love that keeps us in being at every instant. Everything in our lives was and is arranged by him for us and for our salvation.

This awareness of the infinite-eternal Love of the Father in our lives is something that grows over time. We come back to it at set times daily till it becomes habitual and integrated within our everyday routine. From feeling the Love of the Father, we converse with him all the time. We cannot learn swimming simply by reading a manual. We have to jump in the water.

Now is the Acceptable Time

"We appeal to you not to receive the grace of God in vain. For he says: 'In an acceptable time I heard you, and on the day of salvation I helped you.' Behold, *now* is a very acceptable time; behold, *now* is the day of salvation." (2 *Corinthians* 6:1-2)

"But seek first the kingdom (of God) and his righteousness, and all these things will be given you besides. *Do not worry about tomorrow*; tomorrow will take care of itself." (*Matthew* 6:33-4)

"Cast *all your worries* upon him because he cares for you." (1 *Peter* 5:7)

"*Come to me*, all you who labor and are burdened, and *I will give you rest*." (*Matthew* 11:28)

"For God will hide me in his shelter in time of trouble, He will conceal me in the cover of his tent; and set me high upon a rock. ... *Wait for the LORD*, take courage; *be stouthearted*, wait for the LORD!" (*Psalm* 27:5, 14)

The time in the Secret Place is always the state of being present with and in the Father. The divine Time is God's Now not our yesterday or tomorrow or even our today. We should not spend an instant regretting the past, fearing the future or discouraged by the present. "Do not worry about tomorrow." "Now is the day of salvation." The Father is in with us here and now but in his Now. Our eternity is tied to being with him in his Now.

We are meant to be where we are right here and right now. Instead of moping over what would have been or desiring what could have been or dreading what might yet be ahead, we should be doing what the Father wants of us now in his Presence and Power. Our present should be being present with him. He will take care of everything if we "rest" in him while going about our daily duties.

"Seek first the kingdom (of God) and his righteousness, and all these things will be given you besides." This is our blueprint for living in the divine Now.

Living in the divine Time, while dwelling in the divine Space, calls for patience and perseverance, stout-heartedness and serenity. When "a thousand fall at your side, ten thousand at your right hand," we should not fear for "near you it shall not come."

When crises and catastrophes, travails and tragedies strike, we should place them all in the hands of the Father asking him to resolve them. We must constantly cast all our worries upon him "because he cares" for us infinitely and eternally and "will never allow" us "to stumble."

"*Because he cares.*" He is the Good Shepherd in search of the one lost sheep, the Father who rushes to embrace his child-gone-astray, the infinite Lover who numbers every hair on our heads. He loves you as if you are only person who ever existed. With all the effort in the world we cannot achieve what lies beyond our capabilities. But with no effort at all the Father achieves anything and everything we need. So why not turn over all our problems to him who has promised to resolve them for us? He is ready, willing and able.

Meanwhile, we must persevere, in total trust without doubt or worry, in prayer and all those actions we need to take. And we should be patient. We should "wait for the Lord" and "be stouthearted" with no expectation of HOW he will resolve the matter but only the certainty that he WILL resolve it – in the fullness of time, HIS TIME.

In the midst of the most terrifying calamity, stranded in the unforgiving desert, paralyzed by a sudden stroke, left penniless without any means of support, he will come to our rescue if we let him. We simply close our eyes and entrust ourselves and our plight to him. We admit the magnitude of the crisis and then ask him to see us through. "In God I trust, I do not fear."

Patience, perseverance and stoutheartedness are key. Psalm 27 repeats the promise of safety in the Secret Place "in time of trouble." Commentators point out that this promise is accompanied by a call for patience – "Wait for the Lord." And between the two pleas to "wait for the Lord," it asks us to be courageous and "stout-hearted."

> "For God will hide me in his shelter in time of trouble, He will conceal me in the cover of his tent; and set me high upon a rock. ... **Wait for the LORD**, take courage; **be stouthearted**, *wait for the LORD!*" (*Psalm 27:5, 14*)

We remember the other biblical injunctions to "guard the heart." *We* must trust. *We* must be fear-free. And *we* must be patient. God will do the rest!

The Secret Place is our Home. To leave it by deciding to "do our own thing" is to be vulnerable to the attacks of our enemies both spiritual and physical as well as our own weaknesses. Our choice is between living in either the Shadow of Death or the Shadow of the Father. Once we choose to live in the Shelter, the Secret Place of the Most High, we receive his divine Energy. The dark clouds that surround us drift away when we rest in his Presence, filled with his Power.

I am now in the Father. Not just with him but in him. My focus is on him. No worry about future tribulation, no fear, no anxiety. All is calm. All is peace. Everything is in his Hands. I dwell in him. I rest in the Secret Place. A state of mind, yes, but beyond that a state of being. Being in the Father and in his peace that "surpasses all understanding." For Thine is the Kingdom, the Power and the Glory forever and ever.

A MAP OF GODSPACE

We have discovered the Father but our challenge is to live as his children in GodSpace. We need a how-to manual, a set of rules and a handbook of tips. In short, we need a map of GodSpace.

We have created just such a map below charting the three kinds of terrain we will encounter in GodSpace:

- Badlands – *Sin* – making the choices and actions that the Father expects of us
- Highlands – *Prayer* – opening up our communication channels with the Father
- Lowlands – *Worry* – letting the Father take control of our lives, our crises, our needs and our goals

Finally, we will consider two key landmarks on our journey to the Father:

- The role of the New Eve, the Mother of all keep God's commandments
- The appropriate way to pray to the Trinity.

We begin with the role of GodSpace as a portal to the Promised Land.

Parallel Universe – A Portal to the Promised Land

The Old and New Testaments speak of a new God-world with its own space and time paralleling the physical space and time in which we live and move and have our being. We are asked to seek safety by dwelling in "the secret place" of God.

> "You who dwell in the shelter of the Most High, who abide in the shade of the Almighty, Say to the LORD, "My refuge and fortress, my God in whom I trust." He will rescue you from the fowler's snare, from the destroying plague." (*Psalm* 91:1-2)

> "For God will hide me in his shelter in time of trouble, He will conceal me in the cover of his tent; and set me high upon a rock." (*Psalm* 27:5)
>
> "Remain in me, as I remain in you." (*John* 15:4)

In this divine space and time, we are asked to wait on God our Father, to focus on the "now" and not be fearful about tomorrow.

What do we mean by space and time? In our everyday life, space is the *network of relationships* among physical things that involves location, distance and paths of motion. Time is the measurement of *changes in this physical network*.

God is outside terrestrial space and time. What we call the "divine" space is not a physical space or place. It is *a relationship network made up of the Father and us* where we meet Heart2heart. It is a "secret place" located "in the Father." The Father's action in the divine space follows "divine" time: it is not a matter of past, present and future *but our presence with and in him*. Since we dwell in the divine Now, we are told to focus only on this Now – "Do not worry about tomorrow."

To live in the Father's presence, to live by his Providence, is to live in his Space and Time. We have to move out of our space into God's "space." We have to move out of our time into God's "time." Herein lies perpetual peace and unspeakable joy.

GodSpace is a piece of Heaven on earth. It is the portal to our Promised Land.

We will now begin our exploration of its terrain.

Badlands – *Sin*

> *"I am the true vine, and my Father is the vine grower. He takes away every branch in me that does not bear fruit, and every one that does he prunes so that it bears more fruit. You are already pruned because of the word that I spoke to you. Remain in me, as I remain in you. Just as a branch cannot bear fruit on its own unless it remains on the vine, so neither can you unless you remain in me. I am the vine, you are the branches. Whoever remains in me and I in him will bear much fruit, because without me you can do nothing. Anyone who does not remain in me will be thrown out like a branch and wither; people will gather them and throw them into a fire and they will be burned. If you remain in me and my words remain in you, ask for whatever you want and it will be done for you. By this is my Father glorified, that you bear much fruit and become my disciples. As the Father loves me, so I also love you. Remain in my love. If you keep my commandments, you will remain in my love." (John 15:1-10)*

Through baptism and our "pledge of allegiance" to the Savior who redeemed us, the Spirit who sanctifies us and the Father who brought us into being, we become children of the Father. But, as we see in Scripture, we can leave our Father's House any time we choose.

Black Hole

Our whole life is a string of choices, free acts. We are our choices. What we become through our choices is our destiny. Unlike all else that exists, human beings freely determine their own destiny. But human destiny was never about just the here-and-now. As all human societies across space and time recognized, the end-game is eternity.

The destiny to which we are called is Heaven, the everlasting vision of the Father through our union with his Son in the Holy Spirit. It is our communion with That which we need and desire above all. But those who blind themselves will not see; those whose hearts have hardened will die. The eternal self-deprivation of the sight of God, the final, fatal heart attack, the loss of all that we need and desire, is Hell.

Heaven or Hell is what we become. The state of our being at the moment of death is its state forever. So how do we get on the right track, the track to Heaven? By becoming children of the Father HERE and NOW. This is the rule laid out in Holy Scripture.

We enter the Father's House through baptism and remain there through the "obedience of faith."

Free acts have consequences. If we freely reject the Father, we create an ecosystem of sin that corrodes everything about us. Sin is self-destructive: staining our souls, twisting our minds, deforming our being. To sin is indeed to re-crucify Christ! "Those who …have fallen away … are recrucifying the Son of God for themselves and holding him up to contempt." (*Hebrews* 6:4,6)

Sin is powerful: "For I do not do the good I want, but I do the evil I do not want." (*Galatians* 7:19)

We cannot rescue ourselves from sin. We are totally dependent on divine grace for deliverance from our slavery to sin. But, to receive it, we must say "Yes" to the grace that is constantly offered to us.

"My children, I am writing this to you so that you may not commit sin. But if anyone does sin, we have an Advocate with the Father, Jesus Christ the righteous one. He is expiation for our sins, and not for our sins only but for those of the whole world. The way we may be sure that we know him is to keep his commandments. Whoever says, "I know him," but does not keep his commandments is a liar, and the truth is not in him. But whoever keeps his word, the love of God is truly perfected in him." (1 *John* 2:1-5)

Keeping the commandments of Jesus is to keep ourselves in union with him. As the Epistle to the Hebrews warns us: "Take care, brothers, that none of you may have an evil and unfaithful heart, so as to forsake the living God. Encourage yourselves daily while it is still "today," so that none of you may grow hardened by the deceit of sin. We have become partners of Christ if only we hold the beginning of the reality firm until the end." (*Hebrews* 3:12-14)

Sin is universal but the opportunity to repent always available: "If we say, 'We are without sin,' we deceive ourselves, and the truth is not in us. If we acknowledge our sins, he is faithful and just and will forgive our sins and cleanse us from every wrongdoing." (1 *John* 1:8-9) "Since we have 'a great priest over the house of God,' let us approach with a sincere heart and in absolute trust, with our hearts sprinkled clean from an evil conscience and our bodies washed in pure water." (*Hebrews* 10:21-22)

In everyday life, we must choose to live as our Savior, the Son who leads us to the Father, has commanded us.

Sewage Disposal

To follow Jesus is to let him empty the sewage in our souls. We must let him transform us, replacing our old self with a new I, Homo Sapiens 2.0:

> "You should put away the old self of your former way of life, corrupted through deceitful desires ... and put on the new self, created in God's way in righteousness and holiness of truth." (*Ephesians* 4:22-24)

> "Whoever is in Christ is a new creation." (2 *Corinthians* 5:12,17)

This transformation is "of the heart, in the spirit" to be approached "in absolute trust":

> "Rather, one is a Jew inwardly, and circumcision is *of the heart, in the spirit*, not the letter; his praise is not from human beings but from God." (*Romans* 2:29)

> "But thanks be to God that, although you were once slaves of sin, you have become obedient from the heart to the pattern of teaching to which you were entrusted." (*Romans* 6:17)

Letting the Father Take Charge

As with everything else, we submit our moral challenges and our spiritual imperfections to the Father. As long as we place all our spiritual and moral needs and failings in the infinitely loving Heart of the Father, he will take care of them. We are never to be anxious about our spiritual growth. Instead, we should have complete confidence that the Good Shepherd will lead us safely through the Valley of spiritual death to his eternal banquet of bliss.

> "Now may God himself, our Father, and our Lord Jesus direct our way to you, and may the Lord make you increase and abound in love for one another and for all, just as we have for you, so as to strengthen your hearts, to be blameless in holiness before our God and Father at the coming of our Lord Jesus with all his holy ones." (1 *Thessalonians* 3:11-13)

Highlands – *Prayer*

GodSpace, the Secret Place, is our home address. But to even enter the Secret Place and then to "make ourselves at home" there, we should be on speaking terms with the Father in whose "shelter" we dwell. He speaks to us in a "still small voice." Only if we respond in kind can we become aware of him acting here and now and of his presence in our lives and the world. We cannot truly trust our Father or overcome our fears, we cannot face crises and overcome trials, if we cannot "feel" the infinite Lover with us and in us. Prayer is the oxygen without which we cannot live in GodSpace.

"Feeling" the Father

One-to-one communion with the Father begins with our "feeling" his presence.

In a very concrete sense we can actually touch, see and feel the presence of the Father in the natural world. In fact, all sensations, all sights and sounds are perceptions of the divine presence. Why? Because the Father invented each one of them and sustains and "participates" in them through his Son in the Spirit. He is not simply the Cause of all things but a Cause that acts and is known through its effects.

In other words, we can recognize and become aware of the divine presence just by perceiving the things around us. This is an act of seeing things *as* created, *as* requiring its Inventor's existence to explain its existence, *as* dependent and, finally, *as* manifesting the Infinite here and now. Just as we see a poem as a poem and not as printmarks, and cannot see it as anything but a poem, likewise we no longer see the things around us simply as atomic facts but as realities that manifest and reflect their Inventor.

To be sure just as physical sight can be lost, either deliberately or accidentally, we can easily lose the "sight" of the infinite Inventor. The face of the Father gazes out at us through all aspects of our daily experience. But to see this face we must be capable of sight. If we mistreat or neglect our eyes or suffer from astigmatism, myopia or an infection, we can easily impair or even lose our sight.

Let us apply this concretely.

What do we see in Nature? Roaring waterfalls, mist-laden mountains, flowers of various hues and colors, grasslands dancing in the wind. Indisputably Nature is bursting with activity at every instant, exuding incredible energy and following precisely structured laws. The merest stone is a universe of particles spinning around like perpetual motion machines. The cells of all living plants and animals are data warehouses sucking in signals and spitting out instructions. Once our minds have truly grasped the universal reality of innovation, intelligence and energy, we are only a few steps away from recognizing the manifestation of the infinite Inventor in and through the intricate order and the ceaseless hum of activity underlying all things.

Every perception of the senses is a perception of something that was quite literally invented and sustained in existence by the Father through the Son in the Spirit. To perceive it is to perceive the divine presence because the energy, order and information present in all things - galaxies, streams, birds - are energy, order and information implanted and sustained by their Inventor at every instant.

So also the unique combination of properties (shape, color, smell) that constitutes every "thing" was thought up and is kept in being by the Inventor. When we look at a blade of grass, we realize that its color "green", its shape and smell and the hidden engines of photosynthesis are just as much creations out of nothing as the entire universe. The Father is not abstract and remote but immediate and concrete. We decipher the divine language with the alphabets of this world. Once the poem reveals itself through the body of print, the printmarks become both medium and message.

Still Small Voice

> "In the beginning of the spiritual life it was necessary to act faithfully and to renounce one's own will, but after that one experiences indescribable happiness. ... I keep myself in His presence by simple attentiveness and a loving gaze upon God which I can call the actual presence of God or to put it more clearly, *an habitual, silent and secret conversation of the Soul with God*; which sometimes causes me interior, and often exterior, happiness and joy so great that in order to moderate them and prevent their outward manifestation, I am obliged to resort to behavior that seems more foolishness than piety. ... If we wish to enjoy the peace of paradise in this life, we must accustom ourselves to an intimate, humble and loving conversation with Him; we must prevent our minds from wandering away from Him on any occasion. When we are thus occupied with God, suffering will be full of sweetness, a balm and a consolation."[1]
> Brother Lawrence of the Resurrection.

"Feeling" the Father's presence is simply the first step. It should lead us to a life of one on one conversation with Father – prayer. Prayer is, in fact, of paramount importance it we wish to continue living in GodSpace. And yet it is a challenge for us with our limited attention spans and fixation on the sensory.

But this is because we forget that in prayer we are talking to our Father, to the Creator of *trillions* of galaxies and *billions of trillions* of stars, to him in whose vision we have been present from all eternity. We can reach out and touch HIM here and now – we do not just think of him but talk to him, letting down our guards, tearing off all our fronts. He is right here with us: just start talking to him as we would to someone who is physically in your presence. No matter how late we come to the game, it is never too late to begin our journey into God.

When we finally manage to get off the ground and enter GodSpace, we cannot but collapse in love with our Father. We can see then why Scripture tells us to pray without ceasing: once we have tasted the joy of his presence and his union, how can we ever stop talking to him?

Through prayer we break out of our "bit" of reality into the Real World of God's eternal vision. In union with him, we see all of history, all of our experiences and memories, from his perspective: we become aware of the supernatural drama, the transcendent meaning of it all. All of life here and now is seen not only as a take-off point to endless ecstasy but as the beginning of this ecstasy: the infinite energy of eternity cannot be held back once we open ourselves to it.

Brother Lawrence shows us how we can commune with God constantly: "If we wish to enjoy the peace of paradise in this life, we must accustom ourselves to an intimate, humble and loving conversation with Him; we must prevent our minds from wandering away from Him on any occasion."

Lowlands – *Worry*

"That God existed before there were human beings on Earth, that He holds the entire world, believers and non-believers, in His omnipotent hand for eternity, and that He will remain enthroned on a level inaccessible to human comprehension long after the Earth and everything that is on it has gone to ruins; those who profess this faith and who, inspired by it, in veneration and complete confidence, feel secure from the dangers of life under protection of the Almighty, only those may number themselves among the truly religious."[2]
Max Planck, father of Quantum Physics

"I will mention another experience straight away which I also know and which others of you might be acquainted with: it is, what one might call, the experience of feeling absolutely safe. I mean the state of mind in which one is inclined to say 'I am safe, nothing can injure me whatever happens.' ... The

experience of absolute safety has been described by saying that we feel safe in the arms of God."[3] Ludwig Wittgenstein, the most influential philosopher of the 20th century

"The knight of faith having set its relations with the infinite, was entirely at home with the finite."[3] Saul Bellow, Novelist and winner of the Nobel Prize for Literature

GodSpace is our Promised Land. By entering GodSpace, we "turn from darkness to light and from the power of Satan to God." (*Acts* 26:18).

The Laws of GodSpace

To remain in GodSpace we must follow its rules:

- We have to reboot and radically re-program ourselves so as to always leave open the channel of divine Power.
- This means making a new start. Starting now, we completely surrender all our goals and efforts, needs and wants, dreams and desires, worries and fears to the Father. We consciously and mentally hand them all over to him. They have to *leave* our hearts and be left in the Heart of God. All we should have in our hearts is God: his Presence, his Power, his Love. This is truly a leap off the cliff of our comfort zones into the arms of the Father – into GodSpace. It is a leap we take "blindly" so that we may "see." But only there can we be safe. Only there can we find fulfillment. Only there can we rest in the Peace of his MIND.
- We have to operate out of GodSpace and not the Valley of the Shadow of Death. We have to pull out all the "stops," all the blocks that choke the flow of divine Power. "Do not worry" – ever. Our worries have to be systematically, totally and permanently eradicated. We have to vacuum-clean worry, anxiety and fear on a thought by thought, instant by instant basis. Not one worry can be left standing.
- If ever a twinge of worry darts in under the radar, we forward it instantly to the Lord of hosts. Simultaneously, we send up a quick prayer to feel the presence of the Father and asking for divine assistance with the matter at hand. If the issue requires us to take immediate action, we should do so with serene confidence that the Father will resolve it in one way or the other. We simply do our part without trepidation or desperation. We should act with the certainty that, no matter how uncertain things look, the Father has already solved the problem. Even when our fears refuse to leave us, we do not let them dictate our actions. While they nip at our heels, we only take actions that are governed by our trust in Father. And once we act, we move on. At no time can we let down our heart-guard. At no time can we dam up the channel of Power.

- We have to focus on the divinely gifted provisions of today – not *worry* about the divinely resolvable tribulations of tomorrow.
- We must entrust all that we do into the mighty Hand of the Father. And then we work with all our might to achieve our goals and meet our needs knowing that we have a Protector and a Provider who is in charge of the world and all that is in it including us and our needs and wants. Those who operate in this mode will soon find that the Father does the extraordinary through the ordinary, the supernatural through the natural. The Hand of God is visible only to those are tuned in to the Mind of God. We do not ever need to worry because we can always trust the Father – and should. Remember we are dealing with omnipotence, the Almighty Creator of a universe that stretches out into tens of billions of light years and that he created from sheer nothingness. He can, has already and will always take care of all our needs if only we ask him and let him. Nothing is "impossible for God." (*Luke* 1:37)
- Worry and trust are equal and opposite acts. We are called to live fear-free lives of total trust. To worry is to drive in reverse. To trust is to go forward to our Promised Land.
- The consequences of doubt are illustrated most memorably in the Israelite journey to the Promised Land. It was a journey that should have taken just eleven days (*Deuteronomy* 1:2) from Mount Horeb where the Lord had handed down the Law. Instead it took the Israelites forty years of wandering in the wilderness to reach the Promised Land. The delay was self-inflicted. Moses had sent twelve scouts to study the "land of milk and honey" for forty days. God had promised the people of Israel his protection in making this land their home. When the scouts returned, ten of them spread panic among the Israelites, saying "'The people are bigger and taller than we, and their cities are large and fortified to the sky." (*Deuteronomy* 1:28) Because of their refusal to trust in the promises of God, they had to wander in the wilderness for forty years. Only after all the doubters had died could the Israelites enter the Promised Land under the leadership of Joshua who never doubted.
- For us to trust totally, we must always be filled with the Shalom of Jesus. This means not being troubled or afraid: "Peace I leave with you; my peace I give to you. Not as the world gives do I give it to you. Do not let your hearts be troubled or afraid." (*John* 14:27). Our hearts will not be troubled if we have an ongoing heart-to-Heart relationship with the King of hearts.
- Mind-control. That is what we are talking about here. We need to have a total conversion of our minds. At all times, we need to be at peace, filled with love for those around us, joy-full, in conversation with the Father: no fear, no anxiety, no speculation about the future. Our mind has been re-booted and re-programmed so that we DO NOT WORRY. We discover that when we are at peace then everything works out. To be at peace, of course, we have to entrust ourselves totally to the Father.

We constantly repeat – even in the direst straits – "In God I trust, I do not fear." When we live totally in a "peace state of mind" with no worry whatsoever, miracles start happening and never stop. But only if we do not fear. If we totally surrender. Totally trust.

Bottom line: we must turn on our grace "receivers." Leave the divine signal channel open. And we must do it NOW. "We appeal to you not to receive the grace of God in vain. For he says: 'In an acceptable time I heard you, and on the day of salvation I helped you.' Behold, now is a very acceptable time; behold, now is the day of salvation." (2 *Corinthians* 6:1-2)

The Father Cannot Give if We Do Not Receive

To recap: the Father cannot give if we do not receive! To receive, our receivers must be turned on. To receive in this instance means to surrender ourselves to his protection and provision. If we do not surrender, he cannot protect or provide. We have turned off our "grace" receivers and can no longer receive the divine signal trying to respond to our message. We have to leave the channel open if we want to hear back. We have to be tuned in.

Trust totally, fear nothing. Fear manifests itself in worry and we are repeatedly instructed not to worry. But why?

Of course, worry is unproductive. But this is not the main problem with worry. Worry is lethal because it negates and neutralizes the action of the Father. It hurls us out of GodSpace into the outer darkness. It snatches defeat out of the jaws of victory. In other words, we may not "receive" what we "ask" for simply because we keep worrying about it!

This might seem unreasonable at a superficial level. But if we consider the matter more carefully, the rationale becomes clearer. When we are in quicksand, we sink even deeper when we struggle instead of letting ourselves be drawn out. We cannot build and destroy the same thing at the same time. Centrifugal and centripetal forces counter each other. When we give the Father our request with our hand of prayer – showing trust – we take back that same hand when we worry – showing lack of trust. We have shut off our "grace" receiver!

Among the greatest mysteries of all is the fine balance between human freewill and divine omnipotence. The Father's every action – in our experience, in the biblical records – shows a Lover who commands and pleads but never forces. He will command but he will not make us do what he commands – he lets us make up our own minds for better or worse. He will plead with us not to destroy ourselves but he will not take from us the power to resist his pleas. He will give us compelling reasons for obeying him but he will not compel our obedience.

To be sure, the Father achieves his purposes in history with the cooperation of those who freely align their wills with his. And he also does all he can do to guide and encourage us in making the right choices. But through it all and without exception, the buck stops with us.

Worrying is a free act. It is an act that signifies a lack of trust. And the Father's beneficial power cannot manifest itself in the presence of doubt and distrust. This is seen in several biblical examples, the most remarkable being the one we have to keep recalling: Jesus' inability to perform mighty deeds in the midst of those who would not believe.

Fear is destructive simply at a natural level. The very expressions we use show why: "paralyzed by fear," "terror-stricken," frozen in fear," "gripped by fear." We lose our ability to act. We cannot think rationally.

But, as we have seen, at a more fundamental level, fear, worry, anxiety, panic, despair are all expressions of a lack of trust in the Father. Here we are exercising our negative power in relation to God. Worry is an act of the will whereby we refuse to hand our crisis or need to the Father. Consequently, the Father cannot exercise his positive Power on our behalf – much as he wants to.

This is why Jesus emphatically and repeatedly tells us not to worry.

Of course, the Father can exercise his infinite power at anytime and anywhere. But even omnipotence cannot do something self-contradictory (which is something that by definition cannot exist). He cannot create us with and without freewill. We are created as free beings and this means our freedom will not be rendered null and void by divine omnipotence.

In his Presence in the Present

Jesus also gives us the best possible system for overcoming worry. Live in the Father's Presence here and now and not in our fears of the past or the future or even the present. Instead of worrying about tomorrow, we should open our eyes to God's provision at this moment. "If God so clothes the grass of the field, which grows today and is thrown into the oven tomorrow, will he not much more provide for you, O you of little faith? ... Do not worry about tomorrow; tomorrow will take care of itself." (*Matthew* 6:25-34). It is critical that we live day by day thanking and praising God for the graces he provides here and now and trusting him to take care of us tomorrow. The Israelites were fed daily with manna from heaven. As long as they trusted, he provided.

No matter what the crisis or conflict, tragedy or tribulation, let us trust the Father to take care of it all. Worry will not solve anything. Trust gives the vision and the energy to take the most effective action from our end while letting the Father act from his. We have to address our needs and wants with all our might while trusting him to address them with his "mighty deeds" through us and others. Much as we rightly rely on human efforts (ours and others), it is the Father's response to our trust in him that underlies and ensures ultimate success.

Victory is assured as long as we are willing to accept it.

Passing the Buck

Inevitably, pangs of worry will sneak up on us or be smuggled in by the Enemy but here too there is a divine system for dealing with our feelings of fear – simply pass them on to the Father instantly. "Cast all your worries upon him because he cares for you." (1 *Peter* 5:7) Never dwell on your worries. Never let them fester. Never let them mutate and multiply. Instead we are asked to instantly place them in "the mighty hand of God" so "that he may exalt you in due time." (1 *Peter* 5:6) While passing the "worry" on to the Father we should not forget to turn to him seeking his comforting Presence and asking him to resolve the situation. The reason we should not and need not worry is that we can trust him to take care of it all.

We do not know when or how he will deal with the challenges we face right now. We know THAT he will take care of them and us no matter what. The Father gives us what we need not what we want – but sometimes both and more. And he will always give us our daily bread if we let him.

Having said all this, it must be admitted that some of us are chronic worriers. We cannot help it. We start worrying from the word "go." Even when we are "sold" on trusting the Father, we lapse into worry when we face a crisis. Worrying seems to be "second nature." Willing ourselves to be positive does not improve matters. *Intellectual band-aids do not work because the root problem is one of our "relationship status."* Our relationship with our loving Father. Only direct dialogue with the Father, only a complete ongoing surrender of everything to him, only trust in his Providence, can wean us off our habitual worrisomeness. We have to live in GodSpace.

Changing our relationship status and dwelling permanently in GodSpace is a life-long process built on three foundations:

- daily reading and meditation on God's Providence in his Word.
- an at-least-once-daily entrustment of all our needs and wants and fears to the Father who seeks to meet all our needs.
- a continuing conversation with our Father.

Once our relationship status has been upgraded to an "infinity" status we can take on all the world's problems. "If God is for us, who can be against us?" (*Romans* 8:31)

These are our takeaways:

- If we want to receive, we must ask.
- What we receive will only be what is best for us at that time.
- Accept that God knows what is best for us and will do what is best for us and praise and thank him for his response whatever it might be.
- All that we are asked to do is to believe and ask – if we do not believe, we will not ask with total trust; if we do not ask with total trust, we will not receive.

For those who have encountered the Father, life without his total and constant Love would thereafter be unbearable. We can never again say "God" without seeing him as our infinite Lover who sends us his Son and his Spirit to draw us into their never-ending love and everlasting ecstasy.

Mother of all who keep God's Commandments

"Then the dragon became angry with the woman and went off to wage war against the rest of her offspring, those who keep God's commandments and bear witness to Jesus." (*Revelation* 12:17)

Salvation or damnation, Heaven or Hell, the will of God or my own will? Yes or No? This was the choice offered at the inception of humankind. Sadly, as we have seen, the reply was "No" and the consequence a tragedy without end. But then the human race was given a second chance. A young virgin was asked to bear the Messiah of Israel, the Son of the Most High, the Savior. She said "Yes": "May it be done to me according to your word." The result was redemption: the gate of Heaven being opened again through the life, death and resurrection of God incarnate: salvation made possible for all who accept the divine invitation.

So, at the outset, let us say this: Thank you "favored one," thank you Mary, blessed and virginal, for saying "Yes". Thank you for sticking with your "Yes." Thank you for silently bearing the prophesied suffering of the sword through your self. Thank you for remembering and reflecting on it all in your heart. Thank you for saving the day in Cana. Thank you for being the mother of "those who keep God's commandments and bear witness to Jesus."

Let us be mindful here that there is one thing, above all, that matters, one indisputable fact that alone is relevant: Mary of Israel's response to the angelic invitation to be the Mother of the Redeemer meant the difference between damnation and the possibility of salvation for humanity. Fortunately for us all she said "Yes."

Of course, some speak of her as a mindless instrument of a puppet-master deity who was pre-programmed to say "Yes." But the deity they speak of is not the God revealed in the Bible. In actuality, these fantasists simply evade what is obvious in the Gospels and in our own experience. They live in their own make-believe universe. Mary could easily have said "No" as so many did throughout the biblical narratives. The Old and New Testament texts are essentially accounts of choices and consequences. There was no pre-programming at any point: simply a trail of tears from the beginning broken by occasional triumphs featuring unlikely heroes and heroines (Moses the stammerer, David the shepherd boy who would be king, Esther, the young protectress of her people, Paul the killer of Christians who became an apostle). In short, life as we know it here and now.

It is precisely because Mary's choice was a fruit of her own free will that her cousin exclaimed: "Blessed are you who believed that what was spoken to you by the Lord would be fulfilled." You are blessed because you believed!

So why is it so hard to accept the obvious, to give credit where it is due, to say "thank you" for saying "Yes?"

But once we get past our self-imposed stumbling blocks, we will discover deeper truths about this "one thing" about Mary. Her "Yes" is ultimately a victory for God. The last word in the human experiment does not go to the Devil and the errant first couple. This would have been the case if redemption was entirely and exclusively a product of divine action. But it was a human person who pulled the trigger that enabled divine intervention beginning with the conception and birth of the divine-human Savior and culminating in his salvific death and resurrection. She may be the solitary boast of our "tainted nature" – but she was our boast. And this means that God's "idea" of creating free human persons could not be derailed even by the concerted effort of all the forces of evil. There was at least one human person – the Mother of Jesus – who freely chose the divine plan (Jesus, we remember, was a human being but a divine Person). We see a foreshadowing of this in the case of Job, an instance of God explicitly allowing his followers to be tested by the Evil One. Their victory is his victory. Mary's "Yes" is thus a divine triumph in the human realm just as the Archangel Michael's "Yes" to God was a divine victory in the angelic domain.

Secondly, the incarnation of God in Christ took place in and through a family: he was the virginal child of a married couple. The participation of the family went beyond the Incarnation and extended to the Son's redemptive mission. In the case of Mary, she was told she would be pierced with a sword as she participated in her Son's mission. The redemption of humanity was achieved not as a solitary act but an act begotten in solidarity because it was an act into which the Redeemer drew his family. The father and the mother played a supporting role in the lifework of the Son of God made man in a manner that was irreducibly distinct from the part played by his Apostles and other followers. They belonged to an "order" of action in salvation history that radically transcended the role played by all other human persons – *they were participants in the mission of Jesus even before his birth*! As the Fathers of the Church recognized from the very beginning, Mary was the New Eve just as Jesus was the New Adam. At the center of Incarnation, Redemption and Mediation is the incarnate Word of God who is Redeemer and infinite Mediator. But united with him, GIVEN by him and working with him in a unique and irrevocable mode is his mother, the New Eve and the Mother of all Christians.

Finally, we need to recognize the foundational importance of Mary's "Yes" for our own sakes. The gate of Heaven is open. But there is no guarantee of entry. No matter what some theologies say, the teaching of Jesus in the Gospels is unequivocal: we have to say "Yes" to him and "Yes" on a continuous basis (see the last section here or just read the Gospels). In grasping the "one thing" that is pivotal about Mary, we come to see the urgency of saying "Yes" to God ourselves.

But this meditation on Mary and her "Yes" is not intended simply as an academic exercise. It is meant to show that the Mother of Jesus is our Mother who helps us with our own continuing "Yes" to God.

In the din of debate, in the midst of polemics and platitudes, let us not lose sight of this. We are talking about a real, live, always-accessible mother. She was the mother of Jesus. She was named the mother of her Son's beloved disciple. She was finally revealed as the mother of all the faithful. And she was seen as Mother by Christians from the earliest days of Christendom. "We fly to thy patronage, O holy Mother of God" said a prayer from 250 A.D. The sooner we turn to her, the sooner she can teach us to do the one thing that is most important in our lives: to say "Yes" to her Son who takes us to the Father through the Spirit.

Prayer to Father, Son, or Holy Spirit or to the Trinity?

We have seen the greatest prayer of all is the Our Father. But this is not the only prayer to which we are called. This raises the question of whether prayer to God should be directed to the Father, the Son or the Holy Spirit – or to the Trinity. The answer is: all of the above because prayer to any one of the divine Persons involves the action of the other Two.

All prayer is ultimately directed to the Father. It is made possible by the redemptive sacrifice of the Son and our resulting adoption as his brothers and sisters and therefore as children of the Father; and it is through the power of the Holy Spirit that we are able to say "Father." Without the Son we have no access to the Father. Without the Spirit, we do not have the divine Life that makes us eternal children of the Father.

As we see in the New Testament, we are also asked to pray directly to Jesus:

> "You have faith in God; have faith also in me." (*John* 14:1)

> "If you ask anything of me in my name, I will do it." (*John* 14:10)

And to the Holy Spirit:

> "The Advocate, the holy Spirit that the Father will send in my name—he will teach you everything and remind you of all that [I] told you." (*John* 14:26)

> "You will receive power when the holy Spirit comes upon you." (*Acts* 1:8)

> "The Spirit itself bears witness with our spirit that we are children of God," (*Romans* 8:16)

> "In the same way, the Spirit too comes to the aid of our weakness; for we do not know how to pray as we ought, but the Spirit itself intercedes with inexpressible groanings." (*Romans* 8:26)

But in prayer in each one of these cases, we are implicitly going to the Father through the Son with the Spirit. We are praying *to* the Father *in* the name of the Son *by* the power of the Spirit.

If we pray to the Son, it is with the Spirit while ultimately directing ourselves to the Father. If we pray to the Spirit, it is because of Jesus' redemptive death with the Father as the ultimate object.

Jean Galot makes an important point on why we ultimately direct ourselves to the Father:

> "Jesus drew his disciples' attention to the Father. He pointed out the immensity of the Father's paternal kindness, his unceasing and never-failing solicitude, and above all the great love that impelled him to send his Son and deliver him up in sacrifice for humankind. This makes us see that prayer must be a response to this revelation of the Father. Since the Father has willed to make himself known to men through the mission and words of his Son, he must be honored personally in his fatherly love. Since the entire plan of salvation originates in the Father, it is to him that human prayer must be addressed preferentially. Worship of God the Father is, in the mind of the Church, and of Christians, simply the echo of the Gospel."[5]

None of this suggests any "inequality" in the Trinity. We cannot forget that Jesus said: "The Father and I are one." (*John* 10:30) and "Whoever has seen me has seen the Father." (*John* 14:9). Equally significant, "No one comes to the Father except through me." (*John* 14:6). And both *Galatians* and *Romans* tell us that it is through the Spirit in our hearts that "we cry, "Abba, Father!""

When we pray to Jesus, we are praying to the eternal Son who redeemed us and through the Holy Spirit takes us to the Father. When we pray to the Holy Spirit, we are praying to the Spirit of the Father and of the Son. When we pray to the

Father, we can only do so as his children because we are adopted brothers and sisters of his Son through the Spirit.

Most important, Jesus shows us that prayer is not simply a matter of words or thoughts but of relationship. Prayer is a conversation of love. It is being present with the Other. Prayer to the Father, Son or Spirit or to the Trinity deepens our filial relationship with the Father, our incorporation into the Son ("I live, no longer I, but Christ lives in me") and the indwelling of the Spirit ("You will receive power when the holy Spirit comes upon you.") Through the Holy Spirit, who is the love of Father and Son, we become brothers and sisters of the Son and thus children of his Father.

Time is of the Essence
Consummating the Revolution

The discovery of the Father is not a secret to be kept to ourselves. The Son showed us his Father and proclaimed the new era of God 2.0 when "true worshipers will worship the Father in Spirit and truth." After our own encounter with the Father, we have a responsibility to become revolutionaries ourselves carrying the torch of infinite-eternal Love to all of creation. Our hearts must be transplants of his Heart.

We can start by encouraging our friends and family to discover the Father as proclaimed by Jesus. This discovery reaches a climax with consecration to the Father.

Our Personal Consecration to the Father

All of us should consecrate ourselves to the Father through his Son and in his Spirit. Consecration means setting ourselves aside for the Father, dedicating all that we are and have and will be to the Father. Consecration here is the voluntary surrender of our entire being to the Father. Consecration makes us holy and sacred because we belong then to God.

We see the importance of consecration to God both in the Old and the New Testaments. The New Testament highlights the fruits of such consecration.

> "To him who loves us and has freed us from our sins by his blood, who has made us into a kingdom, priests for his God and Father, to him be glory and power forever." (*Revelation* 1:5-6)

> "Blessed be the God and Father of our Lord Jesus Christ, who in his great mercy gave us a new birth to a living hope through the resurrection of Jesus Christ from the dead, to an inheritance that is imperishable, undefiled, and unfading, kept in heaven for you." (1 *Peter* 1:3-4)

> "May the God of peace himself make you perfectly holy and may you entirely, spirit, soul, and body, be preserved blameless for the coming of our Lord Jesus Christ." (1 Thessalonians 5:23)

The act of consecration can be as simply as saying and living "Abba Father, I give myself to you totally and forever through your Son and in your Spirit."

Our consecration will be more meaningful if we prepare for it before over a period of time meditating on humanity history's of leaving and returning to the Father and our own life experience of turning away from the Father and then coming back. The milestones in this journey of leaving and return are:

- the breach between God and humankind at the dawn of history;
- the Father's outreach to us through the people of Israel;
- the Yes of Mary, the New Eve, to the Father;
- the subsequent incarnation of the only Son and his Yes;
- the sending of the Holy Spirit;
- our own personal journey to the Father made possible by the redemptive death of his Son;
- our Yes to our *Abba* Father through the indwelling of the Spirit;
- the climax of our earthly journey in the New Heaven and the New Earth.

We should meditate on each of these milestones and then make our surrender and consecration to our Father.

"Abba Father, I give myself to you totally and forever through your Son and in your Spirit."

Humankind's Consecration to the Father through a Feast of Abba, Our Father, the Father of All Humanity

Our personal consecration to the Father is not enough. The whole human race needs to consecrate itself to the Father who loved us into being and sent his Son and his Spirit to rescue us from the death and destruction we chose for ourselves. The end-point of the rescue mission is our return to the Father from we came.

This consecration of humankind to the Father is required for many reasons: gratitude for creating and then rescuing us, recognition of him as our true goal and source, fulfillment of the deepest needs of our nature.

How can be humanity's consecration be achieved? The first and most basic step would be the institution of a "feast day" or festival that celebrates the Father's relationship to us and his acts on our behalf. Christmas is a commemorative feast day that celebrates the coming of the Son while Pentecost celebrates the coming of the Spirit. A feast for the Father would commemorate the Father's acts of creating us and then sending us his Son and his Spirit.

Jesus came to us because his Father "so loved the world." Jesus tells us his Father is "Our Father" and through the action of the Holy Spirit we call him "Abba Father." What better name for the feast than the Feast of *Abba*, Our Father, the Father of All Humanity?

The idea of having "feast" days goes back to Old Testament with such commemorative days as the feast of Passover, the Feast of Unleavened Bread, the Feast of Trumpets (Rosh Hashana) and the Feast of Tabernacles.

Feasts were days commemorating sacred events in the history of salvation. This practice continued in the Christian community.

How did Christians go about "instituting" a Feast? In most cases, it originated as a movement of the faithful. Christmas was first celebrated during the reign of Constantine in Rome from 336 A.D.. Different regions of the world began celebrating the feast in different eras. West and East celebrate the feast on different days because of their different calendars (Gregorian and Julian). A date for celebrating Easter was set by the Council of Nicaea in 325 A.D. although, again, the East and the West celebrate it on different days. Pentecost was a Jewish harvest feast held on the fiftieth day after Passover. It was during this feast that the Holy Spirit came upon the Apostles and other disciples.

Feast days focus on events, individuals or realities that are related to our salvation. When it comes to feast days, we do not celebrate a particular attribute of a divine Person since each member of the Trinity possesses all the divine attributes. But we do speak of a divine Person as he relates to some aspect of the work of salvation.[1] Thus the Father *sends* the Son, the Son *redeems* us and the Spirit *sanctifies* us. And salvation itself is a *return* to the Father.

Christmas and Easter celebrate acts of the Son with respect to our salvation and Pentecost likewise celebrates an act of the Holy Spirit that relates to our salvation.

A feast day for the Father would celebrate his relationship to us with regard to our salvation as Our *Abba* Father who *sent* us his Son and his Spirit for our deliverance and *to whom we return*. The verse "God so loved the world" captures the nature of this relationship to the highest degree. As Father, he brought us into being and sent us his Son and his Spirit for our salvation: this is the sacred reality we celebrate. We are celebrating his relationship to us as OUR Father who "so loved" all of humanity and not his relationship as Father within the Trinity.

Given that we have feast days honoring the acts of the Son and the Spirit relating to our salvation it is not simply appropriate but essential that we similarly honor the Father's role in the salvation of humankind with a feast day.

Jean Galot gets straight to this point: "The liturgical cycle enables Christians to relive the unfolding of the mystery of salvation in its various stages and in its most important events. The Father is at the origin and at the conclusion of the mystery. The entire work of sanctification results from his paternal love and tends to produce, as its ultimate fruit, the return of humankind to him. His paternal role, which is absolutely primordial and decisive, deserves to be recognized and venerated by a special feast."[2]

Such a feast day would help resolve pressing challenges.

Many have a deist view of God where God is distant and uninvolved. Deism eventually leads to atheism. In celebrating the Father's acts on our behalf we would be highlighting his constant involvement in our lives.

Another major concern is the general confusion about the Trinity among Christians. Many have a belief in Jesus without any understanding of his divine personhood. Others have a devotion to the Holy Spirit with no idea of his divine nature. A feast of Abba, Our Father would help Christians recognize the reality of the Three Persons who are the Trinity.

The feast would also make sense of the biblical narratives. Both Old and New Testaments are accounts of separation from God and a return to God. Once we understand that we come from the Father and that we are called to return to the Father, everything in the Bible and in our lives would fall into place.

Above all, the feast would focus attention on the most important truth of all: God's infinite, unconditional love for each one of us and the need for us to respond to his invitation. "God so loved the world that he gave his only Son, so that everyone who believes in him might not perish but might have eternal life." (*John* 3:16).

This is what the feast is all about and why it is essential. The Love of the Father is what we should discover, celebrate, commemorate and enter into.

Why a Feast of the Father is Required in Our Worship

While addressing many of the theological misconceptions about such a feast, Galot stresses its urgency:

> The absence of a feast dedicated to the Father in the liturgical calendar bears witness to the fact that the worship of the Father still hasn't reached its full development. During the year there are feasts dedicated

to Christ in memory of numerous events of the work of salvation, the feast of the Holy Spirit at Pentecost, the feast of the Holy Trinity, the feasts dedicated to Our Lady and those dedicated to numerous saints. However, there is no particular feast dedicated to the Father. ...

Therefore we note this paradox: the Father, who is the origin of the whole work of salvation and has instituted the entire foundation of the liturgy, is not personally celebrated by this liturgy. He who has the right to be celebrated before the other persons is not honoured with a particular feast. ... We have observed that the new worship which Jesus began consists of adoring the Father: and yet there is no day in which this adoration is directed more particularly to the person of the Father. This observation is all the more surprising when we see in today's humanity a growing conviction of the importance of fatherhood. Father's day is celebrated in families: many feel the need to recognize the merits of fathers and to thank them. Even Christians, who value the importance of fatherhood along with motherhood, do not venerate with a special feast He who is the source of every fatherhood and every motherhood.

Moreover, the Father intervened with His supreme initiative in all the events of the saving work and He cannot be considered extraneous to the fulfilment of His divine plan of humanity's redemption. He is also the first promoter of the entire liturgy. Precisely, because He is the initiator of all the work of salvation and the ultimate end of the journey of redeemed humanity, the Father should be celebrated. The liturgy must follow the essential movement which characterizes the journey and the worship of Christ, which goes from the Father to the Father.[3]

An Ecumenical Feast for All Humankind

How can this feast be instituted? Christmas was instituted through a movement of the faithful. The feast of the Father too should be initiated by a movement of all Christians. It is as ecumenical as Christmas, Easter and Pentecost. All Christians agree on the Father. None can reasonably disagree on his role in salvation obscured though it is in practice.

Galot spotlights the ecumenical dimensions of a feast in honor of the Father:

> Instituting a feast in honor of God our Father would certainly be a step in the direction of the reunion of Christians. This unifying role is at the heart of our veneration of God our Father: Christians cannot pray to their heavenly Father without by that very fact being more closely united among themselves of the same spiritual family. The feast would be a symbol of Christian unity and a powerful impetus toward reconciliation.

> In addition, this feast could have repercussions beyond the bounds of Christianity wherever human fatherhood is held in honor. It would respond to the deep-seated aspiration that has often been manifested in many religions, the aspiration to look to God as a Father. The feast would thus disseminate the joy of finding in God, in the father of Jesus Christ, a Father for every human person.[4]

Given its urgency, the Christian faithful across the world should call for the declaration of a feast of Abba, Our Father, the Father of All Humanity. The feast can be proclaimed by the Catholic Church, the Orthodox Churches and the various Protestant denominations. We have nothing to lose but the chains of sin!

A feast honoring our Father would be our own enduring love letter to our infinite Lover!

Epilogue
Happily Ever After

All earthly life-stories come to an end. But those who "become" the Father's Heart2heart Love Story live happily ever after. That is the Father's Promise: "He gave his only Son, so that everyone who believes in him might not perish but might have eternal life." (*John* 3:16). The Son says: "I am the resurrection and the life; whoever believes in me, even if he dies, will live, and everyone who lives and believes in me will never die." (*John* 11:25-6).

Consider for a moment the thought that reality at its most fundamental level is a relationship, an inter-personal, self-giving relationship of infinite love, a Heart. Such being the case, our lives, our priorities, our values, our goals should be re-shaped to fit this template of reality. For those who refuse to live by the "rules" of reality will have to live "outside" it. In the larger scheme of things, persons and loving relationships are infinitely more important than empires, states, revolutions, causes, ideologies and institutions. And by the nature of the case, we who were loved into being will not find fulfillment except in endless love. We are hearts made for the King of hearts. This is the script that writes itself in the intuitions and insights that constitute the religious history of humankind.

The Father loved us into being so that we might enter into the Life of Love of Lover, Beloved and Co-Beloved. Love by its very nature is love between persons. To accept the divine Life sent by the Father through the Son and delivered by the Holy Spirit is to enter into the "Love-Life" of the Three Persons.

"When we give, we give what we have," writes Laurence Cantwell. "When the Father gives, he gives what he is and keeps no residue to himself. When we receive, we take something and make it our own. When the Son receives, he receives everything that he is. The Holy Spirit is the completely shared life of the Father and the Son, and since there is no failure in communication, he is everything they are. Such love is beyond the scope of the human heart, but it is nevertheless the infinite horizon towards which we are being called, and we shall never be satisfied with anything less."[1]

All of us are invited – but not compelled – to receive this eternal divine Life of Love. God took on human life so that humans may partake of the divine Life. The paternal Heart sent the incarnate Heart to fill us with the Heart of hearts that is the Spirit of Father and Son.

"Before" anything finite existed there was infinite-eternal Love, the beginning less-endless state of in-love-ness that is the Life of God. "Then" came three unsurpassable acts of unconditional Love: creation, redemption, sanctification (time-conditioned words like "before" and "after" apply to finite beings like us but not to God who is "outside" space and time).

First, creation – in an act of infinite and entirely gratuitous generosity the Father brought forth the world of spirit and matter.

Second, redemption – when humankind rose in rebellion and rejected its divine destiny, the Father would not leave it in darkness and death. Instead, the Son, sent by his Father, bore the consequence of humanity's insanity and malice by suffering as a human being the vilest and most agonizing of deaths.

Third, sanctification – in order to bring humanity into fullest union with him, the Father sent the Holy Spirit to indwell those who accepted the invitation to love.

Acceptance of the Father's gift of eternal life requires us to become his Son's adopted brothers and sisters through the indwelling of the Spirit. Above and beyond all else, this acceptance is a baptism into a state of being "in-love". It is an opening of the eyes of the heart, a complete and permanent catharsis that rips aside structures and rules, masks and superstitions, prejudices and resentments. It is a tidal wave that tears through all thoughts and attitudes, emotions and habits. It is perceiving and proclaiming the magnificence and munificence of God in all things, it is seeing every person, every being and thing, as God sees them and loving them as he loves them. It is to transform our hearts into vehicles of the divine Heart.

The unmediated direct knowledge and love of God is something the human person cannot enjoy in this life and hence cannot describe or grasp. But we know that the "eternal life" promised to those who say "Yes" is a union with the Creator of this immense universe, with the Author of all the love and goodness around us, with the One in whom all these are found in perfection. We know that such union cannot but bring the highest possible satisfaction and happiness.

All physical and spiritual pleasures in this world derive from the tri-personal God whose infinite-eternal Love is the Source of all joy. They are only hints and harbingers of the final and direct union with the God at "Whose right hand there are pleasures forevermore." There is an almost terrifying ecstasy, a fearful joy, in the thought of such a union with the Inventor, Orderer and Energizer of galaxies and pine trees, sunsets and smiles, babies and giraffes, angels and the Alps.

In sum, if we say Yes while on earth, when we die we will live with the Life of God in the Heart of God. We will have the highest degree of happiness possible for us. And this state of being will never end. The Father's Love Story is truly one in which we: Live. Happily. Ever After.

APPENDIX 1
What About Anthropomorphism, Patriarchalism, Sexism and Atheism?

ANTHROPOMORPHIC? PATRIARCHAL? SEXIST?

In contemporary society, we have emotional debates about gender and sexuality. What was considered normal in the past is thought of as taboo today and what was taboo in the past is viewed as today's "new normal." These debates are not our concern here.

Just as science deals with what is universal in the workings of nature and not with individual phenomena, we are concerned with what is universal in the history of humanity. Here are the universals of humanity that are relevant here:

- Persons
- Relationships between persons
- Parenthood

Persons are beings who are "centers" of their conceptual thought and freely willed action who maintain their identity over time and have a first-person point of view.

Relationships between persons involve the use of conceptual thought and free will sometimes even leading to self-sacrifice on behalf of another.

Parenthood is the generation of a new person that, in normal circumstances, involves the action of a male and a female.

Science, understood as the measurement of quantities, cannot describe, let alone explain, the existence of persons, relationships or parenthood. Personhood, relationships and parenthood had to be written into the "rules" of reality. Because we are persons who enter into relationships, the Source of existence cannot be an impersonal force. It has to be personal and intra-personal at an infinite level.

With this background, let us consider the questions addressed here: Is the idea of the Father anthropomorphic, an instance of humans making a god in their own image? And does it perpetuate a patriarchal culture where women are subjugated by male oppressors? In using the masculine gender are we being sexist?

Certain religious beliefs and practices can justly be accused of anthropomorphism, patriarchalism and sexism. But such charges have no bearing on Jesus' revelation of the Father.

The Revelation of God as Spirit

In the first place, Jesus' "purifies" all previous ideas of God with his again unprecedented revelation that God is Spirit. Right after speaking of the worship of the Father, Jesus says, "God is Spirit, and those who worship him must worship in Spirit and truth." (*John* 4:24).

Prior to his teaching, no philosophy or religion had recognized God to be pure Spirit. Although they had spoken of him as invisible and present everywhere, they still retained ideas of God being semi-physical and even finite. Jesus' primordial revelation complements and confirms what the understanding of God as Infinite-Eternal Being absolutely requires: God cannot be limited by space or matter and still be thought of as God. In addition, it is only when we recognize God to be infinite Spirit, spirit without limitation of any kind, that we can speak of the inner being of God as Trinity or recognize the Incarnation of the Son in Jesus.

Theopomorphic not Anthropomorphic

When Jesus spoke of God as Father, he made it unmistakably clear that "Father" is not to be understood in any finite or anthropomorphic sense. "Call no one on earth your father; you have but one Father in heaven." (*Matthew* 23:9). "Which one of you would hand his son a stone when he asked for a loaf of bread, or a snake when he asked for a fish? If you then, who are wicked, know how to give good gifts to your children, how much more will your heavenly Father give good things to those who ask him." (*Matthew* 7:7-11)

But why use the term "Father" at all? Because it means "originator" or 'source' and God the Father is the source-less Source of everything. So "Father" is not just a metaphor but expresses a fundamental and definitive truth.

As an aside, we should note that the origin of reproduction itself in nature and particularly in humans is a great mystery. Especially puzzling is the reproduction of persons found in human beings. In the natural order, the fruit of the love of man and woman is a person, a child that is a living embodiment of their love. Neither science nor philosophy can tell us how this is possible and why reality is structured this way. Genetics describes codes and processes involved in the system of transmitting traits not how the system originated: It certainly cannot explain how "persons" can come to be or even describe "personhood."

The Three-in-One structure of the Godhead tells us that we are "I"s who reproduce because the Infinite-Eternal God is an eternal communion of birthing and being birthed: Son from Father, Spirit from Father through Son. Every time we bring a new person into being, we *reflect* the beginningless-endless generating and "breathing forth" that is the Trinity and of which the Father is source-less Source. This is revealed in the New Testament: "For this reason I kneel before the Father, from whom every family in heaven and on earth is named." (*Ephesians* 3:14-5)

Calling God "Father" is not anthropomorphic. Calling human beings "parents" or "fathers" or "mothers" is being "theopomorphic"!

No Gender or Time

Also, in talking of "Father" and "Son" we do not imply that there is gender (masculinity) or time (Father *before* Son) in God. Jesus, we note, emphasized the non-physicality of God. The ideas of "Fatherhood" and "Sonship" tell us about a likeness of nature and a relationship of giving and receiving *within* God.

The Trinity is the revelation that God is an infinite-eternal Act of Love, a beginningless-endless State of in-love-ness:

- an Act and State where the Ground, Fountainhead and Plenitude of all Perfections begets all that It is in an Other thus becoming "Father";
- and the Other receives all that It is from the Father thus becoming "Son:" the perfect Image, the "Word";
- and the Love proceeding between Father and Son, because of the infinitude, intensity and intimacy of the "Self"-giving, the perfect and total giving of the Two, is itself a communication of the divine Nature so that it is a Someone *breathed-forth*, "the Spirit."

The giving, receiving and possessing of the divine nature, of the being of God, has no beginning or end, no increase or decrease, no change.

Ending "Patriarchism" and "Chauvinism"

Finally, there is nothing "patriarchal" or "chauvinistic" about the Father revealed by Jesus. As we saw, his very revelation of God as our immediately and intimately experienced Father was revolutionary – it was never found in any patriarchal or male chauvinist culture. Further, in patriarchal societies, men dominate women; fathers are distant and often harsh rulers. The *Abba* of Jesus, on the other hand, is the prodigal Lover: always giving, always forgiving and finally sacrificing the only-begotten Son for the salvation of those he calls to be his children. "Our Father" is not like human fathers "who are wicked." And the Father is the Source of all that we receive: "Every perfect gift is from above, coming down from the Father of lights." (*James* 1:17)

Of course, those who had abusive fathers or no fathers or toxic relationships with men will find it psychologically difficult to relate to a Heavenly Father. But there is a remedy for this tragic situation. We should start not with our negative experience or lack of experience of human fatherhood or masculinity. Our starting point should be the infinite Lover revealed by Jesus and experienced by his followers ever since. All of us are called to become like this Lover:

> "But I say to you, love your enemies, and pray for those who persecute you, that you may be children of your heavenly Father, for he makes his sun rise on the bad and the good, and causes rain to fall on the just and the unjust. ... So be perfect, just as your heavenly Father is perfect." (*Matthew* 5:44-5,48)

There is no question that our experience of our fathers or lack of a father will color our thoughts of God as Father. If we have been abused by our fathers or had harsh, judgmental, distant, short-tempered or cold fathers, it is hard for us to visualize a Father in Heaven who is loving and kind. The only remedy in this situation is to pray to the Father and ask him to reveal himself to us. Let the Father reach out and touch you: "*I will be a father to you, and you shall be sons and daughters to me, says the Lord Almighty.*" (2 Corinthians 6:18).

ATHEISM? A FLIGHT FROM THE FATHER

Modern atheism is nothing less than a neurotic flight from the Father.

By modern atheism, we refer to a phenomenon that sprang up in the seventeenth through the twentieth centuries and not to the disbelief that is endemic in contemporary Western society.

Many people today are atheists simply because they are born in societies that have cut their cord with the immaterial or enter into intellectual environments that have shut the door to the divine. Their atheism is a fruit of sociological pressures and not conscious individual decisions. But it was not always thus.

Atheism is historically and sociologically an aberration and, from the very beginning, an intellectually indefensible position. Consciousness, mind and the self can only come from a Source that is living, conscious and thinking. If we are centers of consciousness and thought who are able to know and love and intend and execute, it is not coherent to suppose that such centers could come to be from something that is itself incapable of all these acts. It is simply inconceivable that any material process or field can generate agents who think and act. Matter cannot produce conceptions and perceptions. A force field does not plan or think. So at the level of reason and everyday experience, we become immediately aware that the world of living, conscious, thinking beings have to originate from a living Source.

This insight into God's existence becomes irrefutable when we consider just our own immediate experience in the light of modern neuroscience. Our brain is made up of 80-100 billion neurons. Each neuron is made up mostly of water and on average of some 100,000 molecules. These molecules change about 10,000 times over the course of our lives. And yet we remain the same at two months old, two years old, 20 years old and all the way to now. Of course, we grow and learn and change but it is the same "I" and "you" that undergoes these changes. So what is it that stays the same? It is clearly not something physical because the physical, as, for instance, our neurons, is in a constant state of flux. We could not even complete a sentence if we were entirely physical. Clearly there is something about us that is non-physical. Where did this come from? Not from the physical for two reasons: the physical is constantly changing, not just the neurons in our brains but all our other cells, and, secondly, the laws of physics have no room for the creation of the non-physical from the physical. So the non-physical "I" and "you" must come from something that is itself non-physical. And where did this non-physical reality come from? It must always have existed without limitation. This is the Ultimate Reality we know as God.

Irrational though it is, many thinkers have embraced atheism. The roots of modern atheism may be found in a few influential intellectuals who forcefully rejected God's existence starting with the seventeenth century. They include Voltaire, David Hume, Ludwig Feuerbach, Friedrich Nietzsche, Karl Marx, Sigmund Freud, Bertrand Russell, Jean Paul Sartre and Albert Camus.

Paradoxically, the work of psychologist Sigmund Freud indicates that the atheism of the founding fathers of atheism springs from their rejection of their own fathers. "Psychoanalysis ... daily demonstrates to us how youthful persons lose their religious belief as soon as the authority of the father breaks down."[1]

In such works as *The Faith of the Fatherless*, psychologist Paul Vitz shows that atheism is not strictly an intellectual matter. Rather, the atheism of many of the most famous atheists is a neurosis.

Vitz contends that the major barriers to belief in God are not rational but neurotic psychological barriers of which the disbeliever may be unaware. Intellectuals may become atheists to gain social and academic acceptance and for personal convenience. But there are also psychoanalytic motives: reversing Freud's claim (inherited from Feuerbach) that belief in God is a wish fulfillment driven by a desire for security, Vitz points out that within the Freudian framework, atheism is actually an illusion caused by the sub-conscious desire to kill the father and replace him with oneself. The well-known skeptic Voltaire vehemently rejected his father (and even refused to take his father's name).

But this explanation is not the whole story. In Vitz's view, it is the "defective father" hypothesis that covers a wider range of data: when a child is disappointed in the earthly father it becomes impossible to believe in a heavenly Father. As evidence for this thesis, he cites the case-histories of the various well-known atheists:

Sigmund Freud himself was deeply disappointed in his father, a weak man; Karl Marx did not respect his father; the young Ludwig Feuerbach was deeply hurt by his father.

The death of a father is sometimes also seen as a betrayal: Jean Paul Sartre's father died before he was born and David Hume, Bertrand Russell and Albert Camus lost their fathers when they were very young. Friedrich Nietzsche lost his father just before he turned five, a tragic event that had shaped his later thought

Vitz supports the defective father hypothesis with excerpts from the personal correspondence of these atheists that illustrate the true sources of their rejection of God.

Atheism is essentially a rejection of the Father. In many cases, the barriers between our fathers and ourselves can end up acting as a barrier to the heavenly Father.

Concerning the prevalence of atheism today, Vitz remarks that

> The growth of atheism is not surprising given the increase in the number of broken families over the past 50 years, whether due to single parenthood, divorce, or other situations.
>
> A significant number of children in these families may have experienced what I call "defective" fathers. These are fathers who lose their authority and seriously disappoint a child through weakness, abuse, or absence due to death, abandonment or other reasons. There will be an increase in all of these types of defective fathers when family dysfunction increases.[2]

APPENDIX 2
Does Abba Mean Daddy or Father and Is That Really an Issue?

How are we to understand the term *Abba*? Theologians today fall all over themselves in strenuously denying that "abba" means daddy or dad or anything so embarrassingly intimate. This is despite the fact that children in Israel refer to their fathers as "abba." Decades ago, the biblical scholar Joachim Jeremias had said that *abba* was "a children's word, used in everyday talk" for addressing fathers. This was sharply criticized by later theologians like James Barr who said the term was one used by adults in solemnly addressing their fathers rather than something as child-like as "Daddy". Barr admitted that "It is fair to say that abba in Jesus' time belonged to a familiar or colloquial register of language, as distinct from more formal and ceremonious language" but claimed that it was "a more solemn, responsible, adult address to a Father" than "Daddy"[1]

After reviewing the various viewpoints in the Jeremias debate, New Testament scholar James D.G. Dunn presents (as we have seen) what seems to be beyond dispute:

> *The evidence points consistently and clearly to the conclusion that Jesus' regular use of 'abba' in addressing God distinguished Jesus in a significant degree from his contemporaries. ...* The use of abba as an address to God was in some degree unusual, because of its note of family intimacy. ... We can say with a fair amount of confidence .... we know abba primarily as a word belonging to the family and expressive often of intimate family relationship - hence presumably its unfitness for the solemnity of prayer in the view of almost all Jesus' contemporaries. So we are justified in concluding that Jesus' use of it was not merely a formal convention, but expressed *a sense of sonship,* indeed, on the basis particularly of Mark 14.36, of intimate sonship.[2]

R.A. Varghese

This storm in a theological tea cup is the kind of controversy only certain kinds of theologians could have thought up. The issue really is not an either/or question as to whether we should line up with the children or the adults. In other words, do we have to choose between "abba" as used by children ("Daddy") or by adults (something other than Daddy!) when addressing their fathers. This debate misses the whole point. Without question, *Abba* is an intimate form of addressing our fathers. As it applies to God, as stressed earlier, we should remember that any finite idea applied to God has to be thought off as infinitely applicable. If we say God is good, we have to think of him as infinitely good. If God is thought off with the same intimacy as we think of our father whether as a child or an adult, in either case he has to be thought of as being infinitely more intimate than our earthly fathers. "Daddy" is not intimate enough!

APPENDIX 3
Human Heart, Divine Heart, Heart2heart

We have spoken repeatedly of the heart, both human and divine. It is important to clarify further what is being said here.

Human Heart

What do we mean by "heart?" It is the "I," the "who", the "you."

Ancient thinkers thought of the physical heart as literally the seat of thought. Modern thinkers think of the physical brain as literally the seat of thought. Both are wrong.

Here's why: Our hearts do not "think" or "feel": They are simply systems of pumps and pipes transporting the blood that keeps us alive. But our brains too are just as incapable of thought and feeling. The brain is made up of about 100 billion neurons. Each neuron is made up of 100,000 or so molecules. Each one of these molecules changes approximately 10,000 times during our lifetimes.

So what stays the same? How do we maintain identity and sanity through this constant chemical changing of the guard? The only viable answer: it is through a dimension of our being that is non-physical. If there was no non-physical dimension, there would be no "I," for the physical is an ever-changing flux of chemistry and electricity.

And the non-physical is all-pervasive in our experience. We are conscious but this property of being conscious cannot be physically described or explained:

> neurons, photons, et al are required for us to be visually conscious, i.e., see: but the *experience* of "seeing" cannot be treated by physics or biology; scientists call the this "hard problem of consciousness."

We have purposes and reasons for our actions but particle accelerators and electron microscopes know nothing of purposes and reasons. We use language all the time which means coding and decoding and meaning-processing, acts that have no physical counter-part: there are no symbols or "meanings" in the brain.

I am, of course, a union of physical and non-physical not just one or the other. I have a body, I have a soul (the latter unifies all the elements that make up the body). And the I is a union of body and soul.

It is the I that sees not my eyes, the I that walks and not my legs, the I that thinks and not my brain.

And it is this I that we call the "heart". By which we mean not the physical organ. But the core of my being, of not just my thinking, willing, feeling but the "who" that thinks, wills and feels.

"Core" derives from "cor," Latin for heart. Heart is who I am. What I have become. The love that I bear. The love that I am.

Divine Heart

The human heart (i.e., the "I") did not spring out of nothingness. Nor is it the product of eons of evolution. Evolutionary theory is silent on consciousness, conceptual thought, the I: physics and biology concern only the physical, what can be observed or measured.

The sciences cannot describe let alone explain the origin of the non-physical. The laws of nature have no place for purposes or reasons or "I"s. The "I" can only come from "I"ness, the personal from the supra-personal. It takes a Heart to bring hearts into being. The divine Heart.

Divine "Heart"? Are we letting antiquated, scientifically discredited metaphors bewitch us? Well, NO.

Serious thought, profound insights, breakthrough discoveries, effective communication all depend on metaphors. The natural sciences depend on metaphor in theory and inquiry: Big Bang, Tree of Life, DNA bar coding, Book of Life (genome). So do the social sciences: unseen hand, class struggle, the Unconscious.

Likewise symbols convey complex messages simply and immediately. Think of the swastika or the hammer and sickle – or the Cross!

But some metaphors are based on factual errors or pre-scientific ignorance. Think of the ancient Greek idea that water is the ultimate element from which all else is made.

What of the heart? Interestingly, despite all we know about its anatomy, "heart" is one of the most influential metaphors in popular culture: heart-sick, heart full of love, "captured my heart," heart-broken, heart-felt, heartless, heart of the matter, heart of hearts.

In all these instances, what is being described is an idea that transcends science and philosophy, culture and era: "core of my being," "I." And if you say "she is all heart" we are talking of love as the core of her being. The "heart" is "I" and in notable cases an "I" that is loving.

Yet is the heart a valid metaphor? Is there a scientific fallacy lurking at the heart of "heart?" The old idea of the physical heart as seat of thought and emotion and feeling?

Actually, "heart" as metaphor performs quite well under scientific scrutiny. The ceaseless beating of the heart is a physical manifestation of our being alive. It constantly pumps blood with its life-giving oxygen and nutrients throughout the body. And "pure heart" is a most appropriate analogy given the role of the heart in separating pure (oxygenated) blood from the impure.

Furthermore: Stress and emotion literally have a physiological effect on the heart; Our heart rate slows when we process feelings of love and compassion; It accelerates when we experience anger or fear. Stress in fact contributes to cardiac arrest.

"Core" of our being has nothing to do with the *science* of the heart. It has everything to do with heart *as metaphor* and heart *as symbol*.

The Divine Heart is the Core of Being Itself, of all that is, of existence as such. And this Core is LOVE.

Heart2heart

So far so good. We have considered one side of the equation (metaphor again!).

But we're not just talking to ourselves. There's a two-way conversation going on. Heart2heart. We're invited to listen in. Even join in.

God enters into a covenant with the people of Israel – the Ancient Covenant. The Old Testament. It is a partnership of hearts.

"You are the LORD God who chose Abram, Who brought him from Ur of the Chaldees, who named him Abraham. You found his *heart* faithful in your sight, you made the covenant with him." *Nehemiah* 9:7-8

"Hear, O Israel! The LORD is our God, the LORD alone! Therefore, you shall love the LORD, your God, with *your whole heart*, and with your whole being, and with your whole strength. *Take to heart* these words which I command you today." *Deuteronomy* 6:4-6.

"Heart" (Hebrew *Leb* and *Lebab*) appears hundreds of times in the Old Testament. It is the word of choice in describing the inner being of the human person. And the inner being of God.

The human heart
"But you have given my heart more joy than they have when grain and wine abound." *Psalm* 4:8

"My servants shall shout for joy of heart, But you shall cry out for grief of heart, and howl for anguish of spirit." *Isaiah* 65:14

"Worry weighs down the heart, but a kind word gives it joy." *Proverbs* 12:25

"My heart does not reproach me for any of my days." *Job* 27:6

"So he told her all that was in his heart." *Judges* 16:7

"You listen, LORD, to the needs of the poor; you strengthen their heart and incline your ear". *Psalms* 10:17

"The LORD is close to the brokenhearted, saves those whose spirit is crushed." *Psalms* 34:19

"Then Ephraim will be like a hero, and their hearts will be cheered as by wine." *Zechariah* 10:7

"Your heart must be wholly devoted to the LORD, our God, observing his statutes and keeping his commandments, as on this day." 1 *Kings* 8:61

"How good God is to the upright, to those who are pure of heart!" *Psalms* 73:1

"So my heart turned to despair over all the fruits of my toil under the sun." *Ecclesiastes* 2:20

"At this his heart died within him, and he became like a stone." 1 *Samuel* 25:37

"More tortuous than anything is the human heart, beyond remedy; who can understand it?" *Jeremiah* 17:9

"The LORD said to himself: ... the desires of the human heart are evil from youth." *Genesis* 8:21

"We will follow our own devices; each one of us will behave according to the stubbornness of our evil hearts!" *Jeremiah* 18:12

"The magicians said to Pharaoh, 'This is the finger of God.' Yet Pharaoh hardened his heart and would not listen to them, just as the LORD had said." *Exodus* 8:15

The divine Heart

"When the LORD saw how great the wickedness of human beings was on earth, and how every desire that their heart conceived was always nothing but evil, the LORD regretted making human beings on the earth, and his heart was grieved." *Genesis* 6:5-6

"I will choose a faithful priest who shall do what I have in heart and mind. I will establish a lasting house for him and he shall serve in the presence of my anointed forever." 1 *Samuel* 2:35

"The LORD has sought out a man after his own heart." 1 *Samuel* 13:14

"I will appoint for you shepherds after my own heart." *Jeremiah* 3:15

"The LORD appeared to Solomon a second time, as he had appeared to him in Gibeon. The LORD said to him: I have heard the prayer of petition which you offered in my presence. I have consecrated this house which you have built and I set my name there forever; my eyes and my heart shall be there always." 1 *Kings* 9:2-3

"The LORD appeared to Solomon during the night and said to him: I have heard your prayer, and I have chosen this place for my house of sacrifice ... now I have chosen and consecrated this house that my name may be there forever; my eyes and my heart shall be there always." II *Chronicles* 7:12,16

"Life and love you granted me, and your providence has preserved my spirit. Yet these things you have hidden in your heart; I know they are your purpose." *Job* 10:12-3

"The anger of the LORD shall not abate until he has carried out completely the decisions of his heart." *Jeremiah* 23:20

Most moving of all
"My **heart** is overwhelmed, my pity is stirred. I will not give vent to my blazing anger, I will not destroy Ephraim again; For I am God and not a man, the Holy One present among you; I will not come in wrath." *Hosea* 11: 1-4, 8-9

The human heart can be transformed by God
"God does not see as a mortal, who sees the appearance. The LORD looks into the heart." 1 *Samuel* 16:7

"A clean heart create for me, God; renew within me a steadfast spirit." *Psalm* 51:12

"As Saul turned to leave Samuel, God changed his heart." 1 *Samuel* 10:9

"The LORD, your God, will circumcise your hearts and the hearts of your descendants, so that you will love the LORD, your God, with your whole heart and your whole being, in order that you may live." *Deuteronomy* 30:6

"They will enter it and remove all its atrocities and abominations. And I will give them another heart and a new spirit I will put within them. From their bodies I will remove the hearts of stone, and give them hearts of flesh, so that they walk according to my statutes, taking care to keep my ordinances. Thus they will be my people, and I will be their God." *Ezekiel* 11:18-20

"But this is the covenant I will make with the house of Israel after those days. I will place my law within them, and write it upon their hearts; I will be their God, and they shall be my people. They will no longer teach their friends and relatives, 'Know the LORD!' Everyone, from least to greatest, shall know me for I will forgive their iniquity and no longer remember their sin." *Jeremiah* 31:33-4

"With them I will make an everlasting covenant, never to cease doing good to them; I will put fear of me in their hearts so that they never turn away from me." *Jeremiah* 32:40

We also see the human heart turning to God
"Ezra had set his heart on the study and practice of the law of the LORD and on teaching statutes and ordinances in Israel." *Ezra* 7:10

"My heart is steadfast, God, my heart is steadfast. I will sing and chant praise." *Psalms* 57:8

"He shall not fear an ill report; his heart is steadfast, trusting the LORD." *Psalms* 112:7

"A contrite, humbled heart, O God, you will not scorn." *Psalm* 51:19

"Find your delight in the LORD who will give you your heart's desire." *Psalm* 37:4

"Who may go up the mountain of the LORD? Who can stand in his holy place? 'The clean of hand and pure of heart, who has not given his soul to useless things, what is vain. He will receive blessings from the LORD, and justice from his saving God.'" *Psalms* 24:3-5

"Because you were heartsick and have humbled yourself before the LORD when you heard what I have spoken concerning this place and its inhabitants, that they would become a desolation and a curse; and because you tore your garments and wept before me, I in turn have heard." 2 *Kings* 22:19

"Your testimonies are my heritage forever; they are the joy of my heart. My heart is set on fulfilling your statutes; they are my reward forever." *Psalms* 119:111-2

I will run the way of your commandments, for you will broaden my heart. *Psalms* 119:32

"'Come,' says my heart, 'seek his face'; your face, LORD, do I seek!" *Psalms* 27:8

"I will praise you, LORD, with all my heart." *Psalms* 9:2

"How can the young keep his way without fault? Only by observing your words. With all my heart I seek you; do not let me stray from your commandments. In my heart I treasure your promise, that I may not sin against you." *Psalms* 119:9-11

The divine Heart is a Partner in the Old Covenant.
Then it incarnates itself *as* the New Covenant.

The partnership of Heart and hearts (Old Testament) culminates in the Heart becoming heart (New Testament) – so that our hearts may become Heart.

"He has bestowed on us the precious and very great promises, so that through them you may come to share in the divine nature." 2 *Peter* 1:4

"As proof that you are children, God sent the spirit of his Son into our *hearts*, crying out, "Abba, Father!" *Galatians* 4:6

"I live, no longer I, but Christ lives in me." *Galatians* 2:20

"Whoever is joined to the Lord becomes one spirit with him." I *Corinthians* 6:17

Jesus of Nazareth, Son of God and Son of Man, was pre-eminently a man of the heart:

> "When Jesus saw her weeping and the Jews who had come with her weeping, he became perturbed and deeply troubled, and said, "Where have you laid him?" They said to him, "Sir, come and see." And Jesus wept. So the Jews said, "See how he loved him." *John* 11:35-36
>
> "At the sight of the crowds, his heart was moved with pity for them because they were troubled and abandoned, like sheep without a shepherd." *Matthew* 9:36
>
> "When he disembarked and saw the vast crowd, his heart was moved with pity for them, and he cured their sick." *Matthew* 14:14
>
> "Jesus summoned his disciples and said, 'My heart is moved with pity for the crowd, for they have been with me now for three days and have nothing to eat. I do not want to send them away hungry, for fear they may collapse on the way.'" *Matthew* 15:32
>
> "Moved with pity, Jesus touched their eyes. Immediately they received their sight, and followed him." *Matthew* 20:34
>
> "When the Lord saw her, he was moved with pity for her and said to her, 'Do not weep.'" *Luke* 7:13
>
> "As he drew near, he saw the city and wept over it." *Luke* 19:41
>
> "While he was still a long way off, his father caught sight of him, and was filled with compassion. He ran to his son, embraced him and kissed him." *Luke* 15:20
>
> "'Which of these three, in your opinion, was neighbor to the robbers' victim?' He answered, 'The one who treated him with mercy.' Jesus said to him, 'Go and do likewise.'" *Luke* 10:36-7
>
> "Then they will answer and say, 'Lord, when did we see you hungry or thirsty or a stranger or naked or ill or in prison, and not minister to your needs?' He will answer them, 'Amen, I say to you, what you did not do for one of these least ones, you did not do for me.'" *Matthew* 25:44-5
>
> "Before the feast of Passover, Jesus knew that his hour had come to pass from this world to the Father. He loved his own in the world and he loved them to the end." *John* 13:1

"As the Father loves me, so I also love you. Remain in my love. If you keep my commandments, you will remain in my love, just as I have kept my Father's commandments and remain in his love.

"I have told you this so that my joy may be in you and your joy may be complete. This is my commandment: love one another as I love you. No one has greater love than this, to lay down one's life for one's friends. You are my friends if you do what I command you. ... This I command you: love one another." *John* 15:10-14,17.

"Then Jesus said, 'Father, forgive them, they know not what they do.'" *Luke* 23:34.

On just one occasion, Jesus reveals his inner life. Strikingly, it centers on the heart. His heart. "Come to me, all you who labor and are burdened, and I will give you rest. Take my yoke upon you and learn from me, for *I am meek and humble of heart*; and you will find rest for your selves. For my yoke is easy, and my burden light." *Matthew* 11:28-29

All those following him must transform their hearts. No transformation means no sanctity, no salvation:

"He said to him, 'You shall love the Lord, your God, *with all your heart*, with all your soul, and with all your mind.'" *Matthew* 22:37

"But as for the seed that fell on rich soil, they are the ones who, when they have heard the word, embrace it *with a generous and good heart*, and bear fruit through perseverance." *Luke* 8:15

"Peace I leave with you; my peace I give to you. Not as the world gives do I give to you. Do not let your *hearts* be troubled or afraid." *John* 14

"Blessed are the *clean of heart*, for *they will see God*." *Matthew* 5:8

"So will my heavenly Father do to you, unless each of you forgives his brother from his *heart*." *Matthew* 18:15

"Gross is the *heart* of this people, they will hardly hear with their ears, they have closed their eyes, lest they see with their eyes and hear with their ears and *understand with their heart* and *be converted*." *Matthew* 13:15

"This people honors me with their lips, but their *hearts* are far from me ... For *from the heart* come evil thoughts, murder, adultery, unchastity, theft, false witness, blasphemy. These are what *defile a person*." *Matthew* 15:8,19-20

"But I say to you, everyone who looks at a woman with lust has already committed adultery with her *in his heart*." *Matthew* 5:28

Jesus fulfills the promise made to his ancestor David, the man after God's own heart: "God ... raised up David as their king; of him he testified, 'I have found David, son of Jesse, a man after my own heart; he will carry out my every wish.' From this man's descendants God, according to his promise, has brought to Israel a savior, Jesus." *Acts* 13:22-23

To follow Jesus is to transform your heart:

"Rather, one is a Jew inwardly, and circumcision is of the heart, in the spirit, not the letter; his praise is not from human beings but from God." *Romans* 2:29

"But thanks be to God that, although you were once slaves of sin, you have become obedient from the heart to the pattern of teaching to which you were entrusted." *Romans* 6:17

"Now may God himself, our Father, and our Lord Jesus direct our way to you, and may the Lord make you increase and abound in love for one another and for all, just as we have for you, so as to strengthen your hearts, to be blameless in holiness before our God and Father at the coming of our Lord Jesus with all his holy ones." 1 *Thessalonians* 3:11-13

"Since we have 'a great priest over the house of God,' let us approach with a sincere heart and in absolute trust, with our hearts sprinkled clean from an evil conscience and our bodies washed in pure water." *Hebrews* 10:21-22

"Were not our hearts burning [within us] while he spoke to us on the way and opened the scriptures to us?" *Luke* 24:32.

"Heart" – The Medium is the Message

"Heart."

Why this metaphor?

"The medium is the message." So said Marshall McLuhan, the prophet of the Internet.

The medium of communication is just as important as the content transmitted – sometimes more so.

The "message" of the medium is the "service environment" it creates (books require printing presses, an environment that supports reading, etc.)

> "Each medium, independent of the content it mediates, has its own intrinsic effects which are its unique message.

> "The message of any medium or technology is the change of scale or pace or pattern that it introduces into human affairs."[1]

> "The world of modern communications, introduced with the invention of the telegraph in the nineteenth century, is characterized by simultaneity and immediate transformation [and therefore has] massive implications for politics, commerce, social stability, education. and interpersonal communication."[2]

And in the age of Instagram, Twitter and YouTube, images matter more than ideas, symbols more than thoughts. We are returning to the mind-set of a pre-literate society:

> sensory and perceptual trump intellectual and conceptual.

Hence the idea of "heart"

Why "heart"?

> Because the medium is the message.

The Heart that is Abba Father, the Heart that became man (the Son), the Heart that fills our hearts (the Holy Spirit) must be seen, first and foremost, as a medium.

> A medium whose message is infinite love.
>
> A medium that transforms our thoughts, choices, lives
>
> A medium that transforms families, societies, the world.

With "heart", we go beyond reasoning and conceptualizing to perceiving and understanding. With "heart," we are not dealing with concepts but percepts.

Another McLuhanism is especially relevant:

> "Of course the content of a medium is important, but according to McLuhan the content is not the programming. ... The real content of any medium is the user of the medium. We are the content of our media. Each medium delivers a new form of human being, whose qualities are suited to it."[3]

The Heart transforms us into hearts.

The Providential genius of "heart" becomes apparent at a second level. The "heart" image is important for the same reason that any image at all (whether painting or statue) is important:

> Because we are creatures of flesh and blood.

God took on a physical nature precisely because we are physical. "The Word became flesh."

We are physical beings not angels. Our sensory structure needs sensory support. Focus on the image of divine Heart and all that it represents: burning love. We need to focus on this to keep sin at bay, to keep our hearts on God. We need THIS image. We need heart.

The love of the Father – the Love that makes us love letters called to be love stories – is aptly thought of as the divine Paternal Heart. Our hearts were made for the Father's Heart and are restless until they rest in It. The Heart of God incarnate *shows us* the Paternal Heart ("Whoever has seen me has seen the Father," *John* 14:9). And the Heart that is the Love of Father and Son – the Paraclete – *draws us* into the Paternal Heart through the incarnate Heart ("God sent the spirit of his Son into our *hearts*, crying out, "Abba, Father!" *Galatians* 4:6). We are called to live Heart2heart.

The fruit of a Heart2heart life is love:

> "If I speak in human and angelic tongues but do not have love, I am a resounding gong or a clashing cymbal. And if I have the gift of prophecy and comprehend all mysteries and all knowledge; if I have all faith so as to move mountains but do not have love, I am nothing. If I give away everything I own, and if I hand my body over so that I may boast but do not have love, I gain nothing. Love is patient, love is kind. It is not jealous, [love] is not pompous, it is not inflated, it is not rude, it does not seek its own interests, it is not quick-tempered, it does not brood over injury, it does not rejoice over wrongdoing but rejoices with the truth. It bears all things, believes all things, hopes all things, endures all things. Love never fails. If there are prophecies, they will be brought to nothing; if tongues, they will cease; if knowledge, it will be brought to nothing. For we know partially and we prophesy partially, but when the perfect comes, the partial will pass away. When I was a child, I used to talk as a child, think as a child, reason as a child; when I became a man, I put aside childish things. At present we see indistinctly, as in a mirror, but then face to face. At present I know partially; then I shall know fully, as I am fully known. So faith, hope, love remain, these three; but the greatest of these is love." (*Corinthians* 13: 1-13)

Notes

Frontspiece

[1]http://mindspirit.com/why-atheism-is-a-dead-end-an-interview-with-dr-paul-vitz/

[2]Mircea Eliade, *Patterns in Comparative Religion* trans. R. Sheed (London: Sheed & Ward Ltd., 1958), 38.

[3]Wilhelm Schmidt, *The Origin and Growth of Religion,* (London: Methuen and Company, 1931), 267.

[4]http://cjcuc.org/2015/12/03/orthodox-rabbinic-statement-on-christianity/

[5]Reinhold Schneider, *Das Vaterunser* (Freiburg: Herder, 1979), 10.

Once Upon a Time – *God 1.0*

[1]Ninian Smart, *The Religious Experience of Mankind* (London: Collins, 1969) 53-55.

[2]John S. Mbiti, *Introduction to African Religion* (New York: Praeger Publishers, 1975), 17.

[3]http://worshipspot.blogspot.com/2005/04/sacrifice-by-renowned-hindu-scholar.html. Koshy Abraham, *Prajapathiyagam* (Cochin, Kerala: Mantra Publishers, 2009).

[4]Chan Kei Thong, *Faith of Our Fathers – God in Ancient China* (Shanghai, China: Orient Publishing Group, 2006), 164.

[5]Ibid., 175.

[6] Ibid., 317-9.

[7]Walter Burkert, *Homo Necans: The Anthropology of Ancient Greek Sacrificial Ritual and Myth*, transl. Peter Bing (Berkeley, California: University of California Press, 1983), 9-10.

The Fullness of Time – *Proclaiming God 2.0*

[1] Gilles Emery, *Trinity in Aquinas* (Ann Arbor, MI: Sapientia Press, 2003), 197.

[2] Louis Bouyer, *The Invisible Father* (Edinburgh: T&T Clark, 1999), 231. Bouyer goes on to say,

"But ... the very fact that God, the God of the biblical Word spoken fully in the Gospel, is Father, and a Father not accidentally but essentially, has a twofold necessary implication. Firstly, his Son, the Son, is essential to his life, his eternal subsistence as Father. Then, the Son is one with him in his term, in his eternal self-realization, just as he is in his principle or origin. This "coincidence" of the Son with the Father ... has its expression, ... its eternal realization, in that Spirit of life who proceeds from the Father at the same time as the latter begets the Son, and who rests eternally on the Son as the Gift par excellence, the Gift of self-giving."

[3] "The Father as the Source of the Whole Trinity", Augustinians of the Assumption, January 1996, 36-43.

[4] *De Trinitate* 6, 12.

[5] Alon Goshen-Gottstein, "God the Father in Rabbinic Judaism and Christianity: Transformed Background or Common Ground?" https://elijah-interfaith.org/wp-content/uploads/2015/10/God_the_father_in_Rabbinic_Judaism_and_C.pdf

[6] Wilhelm Schmidt, *The Origin and Growth of Religion,* p.267 (London: Methuen and Company, 1931), 268,

[7] Aloysius Lugira, *African Religion* (New York: Facts on File, 1999), 47.

[8] James D.G. Dunn, *Christology in the Making* (London: SCM Press, second ed.1989), 27-8.

[9] Ibid., 27.

[10] http://therhino.org.uk/other/bauckhamwp/wp-content/uploads/2018/11/Prodigal-Son.pdf.

[11] Alon Goshen-Gottstein, op cit.

Time Out – *Exploring God 2.0*

[1] Pinchas Lapide, *The Resurrection of Jesus – A Jewish Perspective* (Minneapolis: Augsburg Publishing House), 1983, 125-6.

[2] Ludwig Wittgenstein, *Culture and Value,* transl. Peter Winch (Oxford: Blackwell, 1980),33.

[3] http://bit.ly/1YEOKVl

[4] http://bit.ly/1PpPRph

[5] Michael Dummett, "The Impact of Scriptural Studies on the Content of Catholic Belief," in *Hermes and Athena: Biblical Exegesis and Philosophical Theology* edited by Eleonore Stump and Thomas P. Flint (Notre Dame, Indiana: University of Notre Dame Press, 1993), 3-22.

[6] Eric McLuhan and Jacek Szklarek, Eds., *The Medium and the Light: Reflections on Religion* (Toronto: Stoddart, 1999), 82.

[7] http://bit.ly/1VpClVf

[8] http://bit.ly/1whIfuj

Time for a Change – *Discovering God 2.0*

[1] Stanley Jaki, *Why Believe in Jesus* (Pinckney, Michigan: Real View Books, 2002), 46-9.

A Time for Action – *Homo Sapiens 2.0*

[1] Brother Lawrence of the Resurrection, *The Practice of the Presence of God*, translated by John J. Delaney (New York: Image Books, 1977), p. 110.

[2] Gerhard Staguhn, *God's Laughter: Man and His Cosmos* (New York: Harper Collins: 1992), 152.

[3] "Wittgenstein's Lecture on Ethics," *Philosophical Review*, January 1965, 8,10.

[4] Saul Bellow, *Mr. Sammler's Planet* (New York: Penguin, 1971), p.52.

[5] Jean Galot, *Abba Father We Long to See Your Face* (New York: Alba House, 1992), 216.

Time is of the Essence – *Consummating the Revolution*

[1] Although all Three divine Persons are involved in creation, redemption and sanctification, we talk of the Father as Creator, the Son as Redeemer and the Spirit as Sanctifier. The reason for this is explained further below.

Every act of God as it relates to the world is an act of the Trinity and reflects the Trinitarian being of God. But certain divine attributes are associated with each divine Person because of an affinity between the attribute and that Person. This is called the doctrine of appropriation.

Power is associated with the Father who he has no beginning, Wisdom with the Son who is Logos (Word), Goodness with the Spirit who is Love. But none of these attributes are exclusive to the Person with which it is associated. Each divine Person has all the perfections and powers of the divine nature in its entirety.

Nevertheless the resemblance between the attribute and the Person's state in the intra-Trinitarian relationship justifies the association. Thus creation is associated with the Father, redemption with the Son, sanctification with the Spirit. The rationale for this association is that the acts or attributes resemble a property of the Person. For instance, creation is attributed to the Father because he is the beginning without a beginning. But, even here, as we will see, each of creation, redemption and sanctification involve the participation of the Three Persons.

[2] Jean Galot, *Abba Father We Long to See Your Face* (New York: Alba House, 1992), 225.

[3] Jean Galot, "The new worship of the Father", December 1999.

[4] Jean Galot, op cit., 231-2.

Epilogue – *Happily Ever After*

[1] Laurence Cantwell, *The Theology of the Trinity* (Notre Dame, Indiana: Fides, 1969), 87.

Appendix 1 – **What About Anthropomorphism, Patriarchalism, Sexism and Atheism?**

[1] Sigmund Freud, *Leonardo da Vinci* (New York: Vintage/Random House, 1947), 93

[2] http://mindspirit.com/why-atheism-is-a-dead-end-an-interview-with-dr-paul-vitz/

Appendix 2 – **Does Abba Mean Daddy or Father and Is That Really an Issue?**

[1] James Barr, *Journal of Theological Studies*, vol. 39, 1988, 46.

[2] James D.G. Dunn, *Christology in the Making* (London: SCM Press, second ed.1989), 27-8.

Appendix 3 – **Human Heart, Divine Heart, Heart2heart**

[1] Marshall McLuhan, *Understanding Media*, (New York: McGraw Hill, 1964), 8.
[2] Michael W. Higgins, "Prophet of the Electric Age", *Commonweal*, October 7, 2011.
[3] http://archive.wired.com/wired/archive/4.01/saint.marshal_pr.html

www.ingramcontent.com/pod-product-compliance
Lightning Source LLC
Chambersburg PA
CBHW070914080526
44589CB00013B/1295